Something To Hold On To

Studies in 1st & 2nd Peter

Table of Contents

Preface

An old and well-liked hymn says:

Time is filled with swift transition—
Naught of earth unmoved can stand—
Build your hopes on things eternal,
Hold to God's unchanging hand.

It is not hard to understand that this sentiment has been precious to the people of God in every age. No less than an apostle warned that all who live godly lives will have to pay a price for their faithfulness (2 Tim. 3:12). Christians of the first three centuries of the church had to endure physical abuse, imprisonment, and even death; Christians of the present time are more likely to suffer social pressures, verbal abuse, and a sense of alienation from a world which is becoming more and more anti-Christian every day.

The Christian needs something "unmoved" and "unchanging." He needs an anchor for his soul.

The epistles of 1 and 2 Peter were written to emphasize this truth. Beyond that, they were written for the purpose of identifying the permanent values and immutable truths which are the foundation of Christian living. They are designed to give the saints *something to hold on to.*

May God bless the study of this book as a means of identifying and applying to modern readers the messages of these ancient documents. May those who read and study its pages be encouraged to hold to God's unchanging hand.

Rubel Shelly

Chapter One

From Shifting Sand to Solid Rock

1 Peter 1:1-2; 2 Peter 1:1-2

First and Second Peter were written to encourage Christians to be faithful to the Lord while undergoing trials. "However, if you suffer as a Chirstian, do not be ashamed, but praise God that you bear that name" (1 Pet. 4:16).

It seems that the particular threat in view in 1 Peter was *persecution,* and the primary menace in mind in 2 Peter was *false teachers.* But the theme of both is the same: Hold on. Keep the faith. Don't turn back.

First and Second Peter were written to give the Christians *something to hold on to.*

Does someone wonder whether it is worth the struggle to follow Christ under less-than-ideal circumstances? The blessings of God for his faithful people are discussed in 1 Peter 1:3-2:10. Is someone having a problem understanding his duty as a Christian to the world, the government, or some other entity? First Peter 2:11-4:11 surveys a number of these relationships and gives specific counsel about them. What can be said to people who are about to undergo a severe testing of their faith? First Peter 4:12-5:11 contains Spirit-given guidance designed to produce steadfastness.

1

What can be done when the purity of the church is being threatened by inroads of error? The nature of true knowledge and the way to respond to false teachers are dealt with in 2 Peter 1:3-2:22. What one doctrine will be most comforting to people facing all these problems? Second Peter 3 closes the two epistles with a ringing declaration of the certainty of the second coming of Jesus Christ.

As the Holy Spirit saw to the writing of these two letters, he was giving their original readers (and their spiritual descendants) precise facts, threats, assurances, and instructions they needed to meet the tests that lay ahead. He was giving them substantive information around which they could build a Christ-like faith and life. He was giving them *something to hold on to*.

Every life has to have some concrete values and stabilizing commitments, or that person will become a "double-minded man, unstable in all his ways" (Jas. 1:8). Yet most people seem unable to come up with anything worth holding to, unable to find anything that gives real meaning to their lives. Our twentieth-century world has lost its sense of goal and purpose. The people of our time cannot agree on the right and good, therefore they cannot unite to seek after them. Lacking a goal for living, there is no motivation for developing character among them. Christians are different.

Christians have been given the means to triumphant living. We have a strong, secure, and unshakable foundation for our souls. We have *something to hold on to*.

In the thirteen chapters of this book, we will seek to understand how Peter's epistles accomplished their purpose among saints of the first century. We shall also seek to apply the truths which met their needs to our situation in this day and time. The goal of such a study is to stimulate Christians to a deeper spiritual resolve in the face of problems and to a more consistent living of the faith we have professed.

A Look at the Author

The ultimate author of all Scripture is deity (cf. 2 Tim. 3:16-17). In the production of the Bible, however, God did not select the human writers he used in a random and capricious manner. To the contrary, he always chose the person whose personal background and temperament best equipped him for a particular situation. For example, he chose a man whose heart had been broken by an unfaithful wife to communicate to Old Testament Israel the grief he felt because of that nation's betrayal of his love (cf. Hosea).

Who was the man selected to write these epistles? What was there about him that made him particularly suited for the task?

Both epistles were written by the same man. "Peter, an apostle of Jesus Christ ..." (1 Pet. 1:1a). "Simon Peter, a servant and apostle of Jesus Christ ..." (2 Pet. 1:1a).

Hardly anyone among the first-century saints would have been more widely known than this man. Peter (also known as Simon, Mark 1:16; Simon Bar-Jonah or Simon the son of Jonah, Matt. 16:17; Symeon, Acts 15:14; and Cephas, John 1:42) was one of the earliest of Jesus' disciples during his time of earthly ministry. He learned of the Messiah through his brother, Andrew (cf. John 1:41-42). Later these two brothers, along with their partners in a fishing business (i.e., James and John), were called by the Lord to be "fishers of men" (Luke 5:9-11).

In all four lists of the apostles (Matt. 10:2-4; Mark 3:16-19; Luke 6:14-16; Acts 1:13), Peter's name appears first. Material about him is found in all four Gospels, and he is mentioned in the writings of Paul more than once. There is no doubt that he occupied a place of high regard in the hearts of the people of the first-century church. Paul called him one of the "pillars" of the church at Jerusalem (Gal. 2:9).

The name "Peter" means rock or stone. And it would appear that Peter was in fact a rock – a stabilizing force, a man of firm faith – when he wrote these epistles. Heaven chose a man who was strong and stable to encourage others to an unshakable commitment to Christ.

But Peter was not always this way. At certain points in his earlier life, he had been much more like shifting sand than solid rock. A great transformation had occurred in his life, and this is likely the reason he was chosen to write these letters. The people reading his epistles would know how Peter had come from weakness to strength. They could identify with his experience and believe that the same power working in them could produce the same effect it had already produced in him.

When we read of Peter in the Gospels, he appears at times to be a giant among men and at others a dwarf. He was not always the stable and dependable person his name indicates. For example, in a familiar passage from Matthew 16, Peter is the apostle who makes the wonderful confession of faith in Jesus, "You are the Christ, the Son of the living God" (v. 16). In the very same chapter, however, he protested against Jesus' predictions regarding his death and was the object of a stinging rebuke. "Jesus turned and said to Peter, 'Get behind me, Satan! You are a stumbling block to me; you do not have in mind the things of God, but the things of men'" (v. 23). What a contrast to the beautiful benediction Jesus had pronounced following his confession of faith.

At that point Peter was unstable. In one breath he could confess faith, and in the very next he could refuse to accept the words of his Master. In one statement he could be God's mouthpiece and Satan's in the next.

Another example of his early instability is seen in his abortive attempt to walk to Jesus on the water. A couple of chapters prior to the episode already examined from Matthew's Gospel, he brashly declared his faith and began to walk on the surface of the sea. But the crashing waves frightened him, and he began to sink. As Jesus rescued him, he asked, "You of little faith, why did you doubt?" (Matt. 14:28-31).

The ultimate example of his instability, however, is related in the fourteenth chapter of Mark. On the day of his

4

betrayal, Jesus told all the apostles that they would be scattered like sheep in the coming crisis (v. 27). "Peter declared, 'Even if all fall away, I will not'" (v. 29). What a bold statement: "Everyone else may fail you, but I will always be there when you need me!" You know what happened. Three times after Jesus was arrested, someone pointed out Peter and suggested that he was one of the Nazarene's followers. All three times he denied it. On the third occasion, "He began to call down curses on himself, and he swore to them, 'I don't know this man you're talking about'" (v. 71; cf. vs. 66-72).

Even the resurrection, the coming of the Holy Spirit, and the establishment of the kingdom did not completely and suddenly end Peter's instability. Paul related an incident at Antioch of Syria where he withstood Peter because of the latter's hypocrisy in dealing with Gentile Christians in the presence of some prejudiced Jews (cf. Gal. 2:10-21).

Through all his lapses and failures, the Lord sought to keep Peter and to use him for the sake of righteousness. After his resurrection, Jesus appeared to the penitent man who had denied him three times only a few days before. They met at the Sea of Galilee, and Peter was allowed to affirm his love for the risen Savior three times. And then he was commissioned, "Feed my sheep" (John 21:7-17). Jesus still had a place for him. He could still be useful. So, on the first Pentecost following the resurrection, Peter preached before a crowd of thousands and unashamedly confessed his faith in the man he had denied earlier (Acts 2:36). When asked by the crowd what must be done for salvation from sin, he was unafraid to state heaven's demand concerning repentance and baptism "in the name of Jesus Christ" (Acts 2:38). He endured persecution at the hands of the Jewish officials in Jerusalem without murmuring (Acts 4:1-13; 5:28-32). And the Lord chose him to be the first to preach the gospel to a Gentile (Acts 10). According to Origen, as quoted by Eusebius, "At the end Peter being at Rome was crucified head downwards, having himself requested that he might so suffer" (*Church History 3.1.*).

As one writer has put it:

A study of the life and character of Simon Peter reveals noble traits. His enthusiasm and boldness are worthy of emulation. He was extremely devoted and committed to Christ. He also illustrates, however, the danger of misdirected and superficial enthusiasm. Some of the sharpest rebukes in the NT were directed at him. His positive traits are inspiring and challenging; his negative traits are a warning (*The Zondervan Pictorial Encyclopedia of the Bible*, s.v. "Peter, Simon," by B. Van Elderen.)

It appears that Peter's greatest strength was his willingness to admit his sin and repent. He never tried to justify himself when he failed. He never decided that his was a hopeless case. Trusting the Lord's love and patience, he kept trying. As he kept trying, he kept growing. And as he grew, he went from being shifting sand to become a solid rock. It was from his own experience that he could assure others that the Lord "is patient with you, not wanting anyone to perish" (2 Pet. 3:9).

For myself, I am grateful that the story of Peter is told in the New Testament. It encourages the rest of us who are only too conscious of our fallibility and proneness to failure. It is humiliating to face up to some monumental blunder and take full responsibility for it. It is also rare. Most of us look to shift the blame to someone else, explain why it wasn't really our fault, or at least implicate someone else as sharing equal responsibility. Worse still, we sometimes push ahead without admitting that anything is wrong at all and compound the original mistake with more hurt and confusion.

Friends hurt each other. Parents judge their children too severely. Married people betray trust. Employees botch tasks. Students fail to prepare assignments. Christians sin. How will you react? If you try to deny anything happened, you compound the original problem with a conscience-searing lie. If you admit it happened but blame someone else, you alienate the implicated party and feel no better in your own heart of hearts. If you try to defy God by persisting in something evil, you will eventually be crushed under the weight of your own guilt.

Peter failed on more than one occasion – and always admitted his failure. That is what saved him, for "God opposes the proud but gives grace to the humble" (Jas. 4:6b).

Peter failed, repented, overcame, and became strong. His faith had not always been equal to the challenge, but he knew the sweet renewal of forgiveness. Now, as an older man who was observing immature children of God passing through the same ups and downs of spirituality he had experienced, who could be better qualified to write the things in these two epistles?

A Look at the Recipients

As to the immediate recipients of these epistles, 1 Peter is addressed "To God's elect, strangers in the world, scattered throughout Pontus, Galatia, Cappadocia, Asia and Bithynia" (1 Pet. 1:1b). The second epistle, with a less specific address ("To those who through the righteousness of our God and Savior Jesus Christ have received a faith as precious as ours," 2 Pet. 1:1b), is likely intended as a follow-up letter to the same people.

The designation "strangers in the world" or "Sojourners of the Dispersion" (ASV) has its background in Judaism. Jews residing outside Palestine were said to be of the *diaspora* (Gk., scattered). The New Testament uses the word in this way in John 7:35 and James 1:1. As the term is used by Peter, however, it is a reference not to fleshly but spiritual Israel, the church, which was scattered throughout the Roman world.

More specifically still, the epistles are addressed to scattered Christians who lived in the Roman provinces of Pontus, Galatia, Cappadocia, Asia, and Bithynia. These five provinces are in the northern part of Asia Minor and may be named in the order that conformed to the route the messenger would travel in delivering the letters.

7

In addition to the rather standard epistolary greeting of both epistles (i.e., "Grace and peace be yours in abundance," "Grace and peace be yours in abundance through the knowledge of God and of Jesus our Lord," cf. Rom. 1:7; 1 Cor. 1:3; *et al.*), Peter identifies his reading audience as persons who were "God's elect ... who have been chosen according to the foreknowledge of God the Father, through the sanctifying work of the Spirit, for obedience to Jesus Christ and sprinkling by his blood" (1 Pet. 1:2). This is a very beautiful way of designating a Christian, for it summarizes all the Godhead has done to bring humankind to salvation. The Father elects; the Spirit sanctifies; the Son cleanses by his blood.

The Father's "election" of the saved is not personal but categorical. He did not arbitrarily decree that certain specific individuals would be saved (and all others lost) without regard to their desires and deeds. This would be respect of persons (cf. Acts 10:34-35) and would make the appeals and admonitions of the gospel meaningless. In his foreknowledge, God has elected (chosen) unto salvation all those who will acknowledge the truth of the gospel by a living and obedient faith. These people are sanctified (i.e., set apart) by the Spirit through the Word of God (cf. John 17:17), and they are cleansed from sin by having their hearts sprinkled with the blood of Christ in connection with their obedience to the gospel in baptism (cf. Heb. 10:22). A good commentary on the doctrine of election is found in Paul's writings: "But we ought always to thank God for you, brothers loved by the Lord, because from the beginning God chose you to be saved through the sanctifying work of the Spirit and through belief in the truth. He called you to this through our gospel, that you might share in the glory of our Lord Jesus Christ" (2 Thess. 2:13-14).

Purpose for the Letters

From the content of the epistles, we know that some sort of persecution was under way against the Christians at the time Peter was writing them. However, it appears that the persecutions were principally in the form of slander (1 Pet. 4:14-15) and pressures to conform to the world (1 Pet. 4:4-5). There is no trace of imprisonment, martyrdom, or emperor worship. The readers are warned, though, that the future holds more severe trials than they have yet experienced (1 Pet. 4:12).

Peter wrote to encourage his readers to be ready for what was about to come their way. Some of them might well have fallen victim to the persecutions of the mid-60s under Nero; even more of them surely suffered under Domitian during the last decade of the first century.

There is a strong tradition to the effect that Peter was a victim of the Neronian persecutions. In July of A.D. 64, Rome burned. Rumors started in the capital city that Nero himself had set the fire to destroy some run-down areas of the city where he had hoped to erect eleborate state buildings. In order to divert suspicion from himself, Nero blamed the fire on the Christians and persecuted and murdered many. Among those arrested at Rome and put to death there was Peter.

If this tradition about Peter is true, both epistles would have been written prior to A.D. 65, the approximate date of his martyrdom. And if 1 Peter 5:13 is a cryptic reference to the capital city (cf. Rev. 17), Peter was there on the very eve of Nero's rage and was allowed time to warn his beloved brothers of "the painful trial" which lay ahead. For our purposes, then, we shall assume that 1 and 2 Peter were written only a few months apart in A.D. 63 or 64.

Our Reaction to These Epistles

Our interest in these two letters is not merely an academic one. We are not concerned merely to know what they may have meant to their original readers. As Christians desiring to grow in our faith and devotion to the Lord, we are interested in making practical applications of the great truths in both epistles to our present situation.

Our world is as unstable and threatening as the first-century world was to its Christian population. We have to struggle against trials in our experience. We have problems understanding our duties in certain situations. We have to deal with the menace of false teachers. We need something to hold on to. We need to find and follow the divine plan for meaningful life on earth. A study of these two epistles can be the key which opens the door to greater faith and purer discipleship.

Conclusion

Contrary to Roman Catholic dogma, Peter was not *The Rock* upon which the church was founded (cf. Matt. 16:13ff). The church has but one foundation, and that foundation is Christ. "For no one can lay any foundation other than the one already laid, which is Jesus Christ" (1 Cor. 3:11). It was Peter's confession of faith (i.e., "You are the Christ, the Son of the living God") and his subsequent life of devotion based on that confession which transformed him into *a rock* of stability within the kingdom.

The beauty of it all is that each of us can be transformed by the same power that worked in Peter. The Lord will be patient with your weaknesses, just as he was with Peter's. He will lift me up when I fall, just as he did Peter. The Lord will give you a useful place of service in the kingdom, just as he gave one to Peter.

The shifting-sand quality of our faith can become firm and stable, just as Peter's did. It is all possible for you, if you, like Peter, will find *something to hold on to.*

Chapter Two

The Hope That Sustains Us

1 Peter 1:3-12

Recently I was reading a follow-up story on some of the prisoners of war who had come back to their homes in West Tennessee to resume their lives after captivities in North Vietnam which had ranged from ten months to eight years. I was interested in learning what had happened to them since their return to this country in the spring of 1973. During the several years that have passed since that return, what adjustments had been hardest to make? Had their values and life goals changed from what they had been before their experiences as POWs?

The story that impressed me most was that of a colonel in the Air Force who spent eight years in a prison camp. He reflected on what had kept him going during that ordeal. He spoke of the solitude and terrible loneliness that he felt. "We were forced to spend so many hours and weeks and months and years with nothing to occupy our minds," he said. How did he survive it? How did he manage to retain his sanity? He said thoughts of coming home "to a good family" kept him going while he was in exile in prison, thoughts which he said "turned out to be completely justified."

Thoughts of home gave that man something to hold on to. It is the same with the Christian and his thoughts of home:

> Sing on, ye joyful pilgrims,
> While here on earth we stay;
> Let songs of home and Jesus
> Beguile each fleeting day.

It is this fixed hope of heaven that has given Christians of every generation the courage they needed to carry on. In the text for today's lesson, Peter is holding the promise of heaven before the weary eyes of his readers. We would be wise to make sure that thoughts of our heavenly home are in our minds at all times. How beautiful are the thoughts of home and Jesus! How strong they can make us when we are being pressed hard to yield our faith!

The Nature of Our Hope

It has been suggested that Paul is the apostle of *faith*, that John is the apostle of *love*, that Peter is the apostle of *hope*. No one could deny that these themes were shared in the writings of these three men, but one would be hard pressed to sum up the gist of each man's writings in one word without using the three just mentioned. And it is with good reason that Peter was moved by the Holy Spirit to make hope his theme.

Peter was writing to suffering Christians. They were already suffering persecution for their commitment to the Lord Jesus, and it would get worse before it got better. Thus he wrote:

> Praise be to the God and Father of our Lord Jesus Christ! In his great mercy he has given us new birth into a living hope through the resurrection of Jesus Christ from the dead, and into an inheritance that can never perish, spoil or fade – kept in heaven for you, who through faith are shielded by God's power until the coming of the salvation that is ready to be revealed in the last time (1 Pet. 1:3-5).

As to the *future*, the child of God has an "inheritance" reserved in heaven. By the great mercy of the Father in heaven, each believer has experienced "new birth" (cf. John 3:3,5). By virtue of this new birth, we have become "children of God ... heirs of God ... joint-heirs with Christ" (Rom. 8:16-17). The very thought of it is staggering. God's blessings to us in this life are wonderful, but they are only a tiny sample of the things that await us when we get home. In fact, the things which constitute our eternal inheritance are so grand that they are not capable of description with human language. Therefore Peter spoke of that inheritance negatively; it "can never perish, spoil or fade." Do things of this life slip through our fingers and perish? The things of heaven are incorruptible (i.e., imperishable, permanent). Are the best things we know on earth tainted a bit with the pollution of sin? The things of heaven are undefiled (i.e., unsoiled, incapable of being blemished), for there is nothing unclean in that most perfect of places (cf. Rev. 21:27). Are the pleasures we experience in this life received with a cynical spirit which knows that they must soon pass away? The bliss of heaven will never fade (i.e., diminish, wither), for everything about it is not only everlasting but also perpetually fresh.

Our bright hope for the future is rooted in a *past event.* God raised Jesus from the dead and made his resurrection the pledge of our own.

> But Christ has indeed been raised from the dead, the firstfruits of those who have fallen asleep. For since death came through a man, the resurrection of the dead comes also through a man. For as in Adam all die, so in Christ all will be made alive. But each in his own turn: Christ, the firstfruits; then, when he comes, those who belong to him" (1 Cor. 15:20-23).

On the eve of his death, Jesus looked beyond that event to his resurrection and continuing work on behalf of his people. He said, "In my Father's house are many rooms ... And if I go and prepare a place for you, I will come back

13

and take you to be with me that you also may be where I am" (John 14:2-3).

Looking to the past, we see God's power and hear Jesus' promise in connection with the resurrection.

Looking to the future, we have the confident hope of a heavenly inheritance. But what of the *present*? "Through faith you are shielded by God's power until the coming of the salvation that is ready to be revealed in the last time" (1 Pet. 1:5). The power of God is working in the present time "to keep you from falling and to present you before his glorious presence without fault and with great joy" (Jude 24; cf. Eph. 1:19). If we let our faith fail (cf. Luke 22:31-32), we forfeit the security spoken of here; so long as our faith is maintained, our inheritance is certain.

As we reflect on these facts, we are made to feel sure and confident. We become conscious of what Peter calls a "living hope." It is grounded in the trustworthy promise of God and cannot fail. When the hopes and dreams of others have come to nothing, the Christian's hope is yet unassailed.

The Power of Our Hope

The advantage of such an assurance to its possessor is evident. The assurance of victory is the best incentive for the weary soldier to keep fighting. The certainty of reaching his destination will cause a tired traveler to press on in his journey. The knowledge that better things await him in heaven will both keep the Christian from getting caught up in the trivial fascinations of the world and comfort him when he must suffer for his commitment to the Lord. As Paul expressed it: "I consider that our present sufferings are not worth comparing with the glory that will be revealed in us" (Rom. 8:18).

To his readers, who were in the throes of a "painful trial" which would put their faith to a severe test (cf. 1 Pet. 4:12), Peter wrote this about the sustaining power of their hope:

In this you greatly rejoice, though now for a little while you may have had to suffer grief in all kinds of trials. These have come so that your faith – of greater worth than gold, which perishes even though refined by fire – may be proved genuine and may result in praise, glory and honor when Jesus Christ is revealed. Though you have not seen him, you love him; and even though you do not see him now, you believe in him and are filled with an inexpressible and glorious joy, for you are receiving the goal of your faith, the salvation of your souls (1 Pet. 1:6-9).

Peter knew that if his readers could only look beyond the circumstances of the moment to the eternal things of God, they would find the strength to hang on. More than that, he knew that they could find reason to rejoice and sing. Quoting Paul again:

Therefore we do not lose heart. Though outwardly we are wasting away, yet inwardly we are being renewed day by day. For our light and momentary troubles are achieving for us an eternal glory that far outweighs them all. So we fix our eyes not on what is seen, but on what is unseen. For what is seen is temporary, but what is unseen is eternal" (2 Cor. 4:16-18).

The trials that come to us during the course of a lifetime are from various sources. There are tragic accidents, lingering illnesses, physical handicaps, business failures, and countless others. God does not allow these things in human experience for the purpose of hurting his creatures; he allows them for the sake of testing our moral and spiritual quality. Every man or woman is regarded as unproved before God, and the trials of life come to put faith to the test. These trials are not evil in themselves, and God is not blameworthy for allowing them. To the contrary, as with the passing of gold through a refiner's fire, these challenges allow the purity of one's faith to be made evident. The Christian who is faithful to God through some period of intense testing brings praise, honor, and glory to the Father; the outcome to himself is the salvation of his soul.

15

The Certainty of Our Hope

Having mentioned the salvation which would come to Christians who persevere under trials, Peter was caused to make several observations about this greatest of God's gifts. He said that this salvation had been prophesied by the Holy Spirit through the Old Testament prophets, that the prophets themselves had studied their predictions carefully, and that even the angels of heaven had an intense interest in the matter.

Concerning this salvation, the prophets, who spoke of the grace that was to come to you, searched intently and with the greatest care, trying to find out the time and circumstances to which the Spirit of Christ in them was pointing when he predicted the sufferings of Christ and the glories that would follow. It was revealed to them that they were not serving themselves but you, when they spoke of the things that have now been told you by those who have preached the gospel to you by the Holy Spirit sent from heaven. Even angels long to look into these things (1 Pet. 1:10-12).

Many commentators have pointed out the implications of these verses for such important topics as inspiration, the Holy Spirit, and others. But should we not look for some connection between these verses and the hope of which Peter has been writing? Is there some logical link? There is indeed.

The Old Testament prophets had foretold things whose meaning they had not fully understood. They spoke of blessings that God would bring to mankind by means of the sufferings of Christ (cf. Isa. 53:10-12; Psa. 16:8-11), yet they did not see how or when these things would come to pass. Fortunately for us, however, the accomplishment of these things was not dependent upon their ability to bring them to completion. The Holy Spirit was in them to give them the messages they spoke and wrote, and divine power and wisdom saw to their fulfillment.

16

Did not the same Holy Spirit guide the New Testament prophets to deliver their messages of assurance about the outcome of events in this final age? Was it not he who told us of our heavenly inheritance? Yes, and he has given us the promise that we can bear our trials successfully and realize the goal of our faith, eternal salvation. "My problem is just too great!" exclaims one. "And how can my situation ever be to God's glory?" asks another. The same divine power and wisdom which saw that all the promises made through the Old Testament prophets were brought to their fulfillment is still at work in the world today to bring about the things which have been promised to us.

These verses speak of certainty. Verses 3-5 explained the nature of our hope; it is a "living hope" which looks to an inheritance reserved for us in heaven. Verses 6-9 spoke of the power of such a hope within a man; it can give him strength to endure any amount of adversity. Then these final verses record the reason why we can look to our heavenly reward as a positive fact; our hope rests not on the word of men but on the very testimony of deity. Since we know that God would not and could not deceive us (cf. Tit. 1:2), the faithful child of God knows beyond doubt what is waiting for him at the end of his journey.

The writer of Hebrews spoke of being "greatly encouraged" by means of the "hope offered to us ... as an anchor for the soul, firm and secure" (Heb. 6:18-19). This is the hope which every Christian must have to face life's most severe challenges. Such hope is not mere wishful thinking but is the confident expectation that God's promises to us will not fail.

Conclusion

Thoughts of home were what kept an imprisoned man alive and sane during his ordeal of eight years in a prison camp. Thoughts of their heavenly home kept many a Christian of the first century strong in the face of wild animals and cruel men. These same thoughts in your heart will see you through your darkest hours.

The Bible calls us to view life from the end, to take what we might call "the eternal perspective" on things. A woman in great pain endures it triumphantly, for she is looking to the birth of her child. A scientist persists day after day through failed experiments, for he is looking for a cure for leukemia. The Word of God tries to get us to see things this way – pain overshadowed by a great outcome, frustrations erased by a fuller understanding.

In every Christian's life there will inevitably come times when the Lord's promise to come again and receive his people unto himself in heaven will have to carry him through some great difficulty. Faith reaches out for strength, and it is hope that gives *something to hold on to.*

Chapter Three

"Be Ye Holy ..."

1 Peter 1:13–2:3

To say that one is a Christian is to say that he is a *changed person*. I come to the Lamb of God "just as I am," but I come with the understanding that I will never be the same again. Coming as one who is unclean, he makes me pure by the power of his blood; coming as a slave to sin, he pays the ransom and sets me free; coming as a son of iniquity, he makes me a child of God. Having resisted God, I now yield to him; having rebelled against his will, I now obey its commandments; having despised righteousness, I now love the ways of God.

The New Testament uses the word *holy* (Gk., *hagios*) to describe a person who has undergone this marvelous transformation. The word *hagios* signifies that which is pure and bright. It refers to things which are in special relationship with God. It marks a person or thing as different and set apart from the rest. God himself is *the* Holy One, and "holy is his name" (Luke 1:49). Christians are saints (the Greek word so translated is *hagios*, cf. Rom. 1:7), and their lives must be characterized by holiness (Gk., *hagiosune*, cf. 2 Cor. 7:1).

19

In the section of text to which our attention turns now, Peter discusses the concept of holiness. Let us study it closely with a view to developing this trait more fully in our lives.

A Consequence of Our Hope

The exhortation to holiness begins at verse 13 with the word "therefore." This means that the appeal about to be made is based on what has just been said. In order for us to appreciate what is about to be discussed, it will be necessary to look back at the verses studied in Chapter Two. The theme of that lesson was *hope.* Because Christ has been raised from the dead, we know that God will raise us up as well; because we have been born anew into the family of God, we are his heirs and have a heavenly inheritance awaiting us; because the promises of God are sure, we are confident that he will keep his faithful people to the end. It is on the basis of our hope (i.e., confident expectation of salvation) that God calls us to holiness.

> Therefore, prepare your minds for action; be self-controlled; set your hope fully on the grace to be given you when Jesus Christ is revealed. As obedient children, do not conform to the evil desires you had when you lived in ignorance. But just as he who called you is holy, so be holy in all you do; for it is written: "Be holy, because I am holy" (1 Pet. 1:13-16).

There is nothing better than a great aim and goal for keeping a man pure, for helping him resist temptation.

Two men of the same age and similar backgrounds were stationed overseas with the military. In town one weekend, they were approached and propositioned by prostitutes. One accepted their "invitation," and the other did not. A few days later, the man who had debased himself asked the other why he had turned down his "chance for a good time." "Back home there is a girl waiting for me," he said, "and we are going to be married when I have finished my tour of duty. She is pure and good, and I could not have faced her again if I had gone with you."

20

The person who knows that something good is waiting at the end of the road will make appropriate preparation. If he is traveling to meet a king, he will take care not to get dirty on the way. Since the Christian is on the way to see God, he has a strong motivation to keep himself pure in heart and life.

As the apostle John expressed it:

Dear friends, now we are children of God, and what we will be has not yet been made known. But we know that when he appears, we shall be like him, for we shall see him as he is. Everyone who has this hope in him purifies himself, just as he is pure" (1 John 3:2-3).

God has the right to expect and demand holiness of us because of his own inherent holiness. Since he is separated from sin, we must likewise abhor and avoid it. Thus he commands, "Come out from them and be separate" (2 Cor. 6:17). According to Paul, the precious "promises" we have from God become the motivation for "perfecting holiness out of reverence for God" (2 Cor. 7:1).

Since God is set apart and different from mankind, those of us who belong to him must also be different.

Therefore, I urge you brothers, in view of God's mercy, to offer your bodies as living sacrifices, holy and pleasing to God – this is your spiritual act of worship. Do not conform any longer to the pattern of this world, but be transformed by the renewing of your mind. Then you will be able to test and approve what God's will is – his good, pleasing and perfect will (Rom. 12:1-2).

The call to "prepare your minds for action" ("girding up of the loins of your mind," ASV) in verse 13 is a very beautiful thought. Men of Peter's time wore clothing which was rather long and bulky, and in order to move quickly they had to tuck the long folds of their clothing into their belts. The "girding up" of one's mind is therefore a figure designed to suggest vigorous mental activity. It is equivalent to the "renewing of your mind" spoken of by Paul in Romans 12:2. Christianity is a rational religion which is designed to appeal to and transform our minds. Emotionalism is temporary and unstable. The settled and stable spiritual life must be based on the deeper power of an intellectual commitment to truth. This life is one of knowledge as opposed to "ignorance"; it is lived in "obedience" rather than "the evil desires you had" in a pre-Christian life (v. 14).

Thus it is that Peter leads his readers to think deeply about God and what he has done for the people he has saved. Such thoughts will not only give one hope and confidence for the future but also purpose and holiness for the life he is living today. As his mind is renewed, his life will be changed and made different.

How Fear Produces Holiness

But there is another element which works to produce holiness in the life of a child of God. Gratitude for the past and hope for the future are motivations to holiness, but so is *reverent fear.*

> Since you call on a Father who judges each man's work impartially, live your lives as strangers here in reverent fear. For you know that it was not with perishable things such as silver or gold that you were redeemed from the empty way of life handed down to you from your forefathers, but with the precious blood of Christ, a lamb without blemish or defect. He was chosen before the creation of the world, but was revealed in these last times for your sake. Through him you believe in God, who raised him from the dead and glorified him, and so your faith and hope are in God (1 Pet. 1:17-21).

Modern temperament seems to recoil from the idea of fear of God. We are reminded constantly that love is the purest of motives and that fear will not be adequate to make a man all God wants him to be. Some have even suggested that the English word "fear" is inappropriate as a translation in this passage, that "respect" or "reverence" would be better.

The fear of God is not an unhealthy thing. It is not a low and unworthy motivation for holiness. To the contrary, "through the fear of the Lord a man avoids evil" (Prov. 16:6b). "The fear of the Lord is the beginning of wisdom" (Psa. 111:10). And the same Jesus who told us to love God with our whole beings (cf. Matt. 22:37) also commanded, "Do not be afraid of those who kill the body but cannot kill the soul. Rather, be afraid of the One who can destroy both soul and body in hell" (Matt. 10:28). The fear which our Lord speaks of in this passage grows out of reverence rather than mere terror, but it goes further than reverence. Many ancients reverenced their gods with homage and service, but they did not fear them.

We fear our God because we know he will judge our works "without respect of persons" (v. 17). In recent years our newspapers have carried reports of men who have committed crimes but were allowed to go unpunished because of who they were. These men had no fear of judgment, for they knew they would be shown partiality. There is no such injustice before the God of heaven. We know that our inheritance of heaven will be forfeited if we go back to the sinful lives we used to live. Reverent fear of a holy God keeps us alert and causes consciences to stay tender. It is therefore a good thing to fear God.

We also fear God because we know what a tremendously high price he paid for our redemption (vs. 18-21). When we reflect on the fact that the precious blood of Jesus Christ was necessary to save us, we are struck with a sense of fear as well as gratitude.

If we deliberately keep on sinning after we have received the knowledge of the truth, no sacrifice for sins is left, but only a fearful expectation of judgment and of raging fire that will consume the enemies of God. Anyone who rejected the law of Moses died without mercy on the testimony of two or three witnesses. How much more severely do you think a man deserves to be punished who has trampled the Son of God under foot, who has treated as an unholy thing the blood of the covenant that sanctified him, and who has insulted the Spirit of grace? (Heb. 10:26-29).

God has loved me, desired to save me, and given the very best of heaven to that end. That makes me afraid. I fear lest I fail to respond to his effort. I fear lest I fail to be holy, to be different, to live as one in special relationship with God.

A Fruit of Holiness: Brotherly Love

One of the facts that impresses itself on the mind of the person who is *hagios* (i.e., holy, different, in special relationship with God) is that he is a member of a fellowship of people like himself. This leads him to a sense of special relationship not only with his Father but with the brothers and sisters in his Father's larger family.

> Now that you have purified yourselves by obeying the truth so that you have sincere love for your brothers, love one another deeply, from the heart. For you have been born again, not of perishable seed, but of imperishable, through the living and enduring word of God. For, "All men are like grass, and all their glory is like the flowers of the field; the grass withers and the flowers fall, but the word of the Lord stands forever." And this is the word that was preached to you (1 Pet. 1:22-25).

Notice first how these people came to be among the holy ones of God. Their souls were purified in connection with "obeying the truth." They were "born again" through the Word of God (cf. Jas. 1:18). When the "word" was preached to them, they received it in obedient faith.

Take, as an additional example of how the word accomplishes its goal, the preaching of the gospel at Corinth.

The book of Acts records how "many of the Corinthians who heard [Paul] believed and were baptized" (Acts 18:8). Then, when Paul later wrote a letter to these people, he called them "saints" (a plural form of *hagios*, 1 Cor. 1:2).

The notion which most people have of a "saint" or "holy one" is altogether wrong. One does not become a saint by means of a life of arduous self-denial and suffering. God makes him a saint the very instant he saves him from sin. In the act of being baptized into Christ, an individual is cleansed of his sin and made *hagios*. This does not mean that he will be made incapable of sin. It means that he is now set apart from other men and committed to live for God in this world. He has been saved by God, and now there must be something of the purity of God in all that he does.

The love of one's brethren is a case in point which illustrates how the very purity of God will be seen in his holy people. Men of the world may pretend to love another for the sake of selfish advantage; men who belong to God love each other without pretense. They love one another "deeply, from the heart." One whose soul has not been purified through his obedience to the truth cannot love after this fashion.

Working Out Our Own Salvation

Negatively, the purifying of our souls through obedience to the truth calls for us to shun some things which would destroy holiness and hinder our growth into spiritual manhood.

> Therefore, rid yourselves of all malice and all deceit, hypocrisy, envy, and slander of every kind. Like newborn babies, crave pure spiritual milk, so that by it you may grow up in your salvation, now that you have tasted that the Lord is good (1 Pet. 2:1-3).

Isn't a Christian already saved? How, then, can one "grow up in your salvation"? The idea here is not difficult; neither is it new in this epistle. Salvation relates to both the present and the future. Yes, one receives salvation from his past sins at baptism; but the ultimate salvation he looks forward to is at the end of his Christian journey (cf. 1 Pet. 1:9). In order to experience it, he must put away evil and nourish his soul on the life-giving Word of God. In this process, one is but accepting the human responsibility which is inherent in Christianity.

"Malice" (wickedness, ASV) is a broad word which embraces all the wicked ways of the world. Most likely Peter intends that we should understand this word to be explained by the specific terms which follow. "Deceit" refers to false or deceptive behavior; it embraces anything which is intended to deceive or take advantage of another person for one's selfish ends. "Hypocrisy" is from a word which means playing a part or acting; it includes all words and deeds which do not express one's true feelings. "Envy" is the feeling of unhappiness which comes to one who begrudges another's good fortune; it is a selfish and ugly spirit. "Slander" (evil speaking, ASV) is a wicked use of the tongue against another's reputation; it is speaking against another so as to hurt him. All these things are to be stripped off, put away, put to death.

In context, the reason why these things must be shunned is obvious. Holiness shows itself in brotherly love, and all these sinful things are precisely such as would work against brotherly love to destroy it. They must be put away.

On a more positive note, we must "crave pure spiritual milk" by means of which believers "grow up in your salvation." Just as we must have food for our physical bodies, so must we have food for our spiritual beings. That food is provided in the Word of God. Just as the food we take for our physical bodies must be pure and unadulterated, so must we receive the pure spiritual milk of God's truth. Human tradition makes void the Word of God (cf. Matt. 15:9), and to leave the truth for another gospel is to bring oneself under the anathema of God (cf. Gal. 1:8-9).

Conclusion

Christians are not special because of *who* we are but *whose* we are. We are special because of the One to whom we belong. Because we are children of the Holy God, we are obliged to honor him with our very beings. We must allow his purity to be seen in us. We must be saints. We must be holy.

The challenge to holiness is a powerful motivation in a Christian's life. It is not so much that we want to be different from others, for it is only natural to want to conform. It is certainly not the case that we simply want to be contrary and difficult, for God wants us to be at peace with all men. In a nutshell, we are forced to be different from people of the world because of the commitment we have made to God.

We will never achieve the absolute holiness which belongs to God alone, but we must be as nearly like him as we can. People must be able to see the change that he has brought about in our lives. They must never have cause to doubt that we belong to him and are consecrated to his service. The daily challenge of living such a life, a holy life, gives us *something to hold on to.*

Chapter Four

The Savior's Special People

1 Peter 2:4-25

It is a constant theme of Scripture that the people of God are unique, separate, and honored. In the Old Testament era, the Lord took a small and weak people unto himself and made that nation an honored and great entity. It was neither their own wealth and power nor the opinion of other nations that mattered; it was Israel's covenant relationship with God that caused her to become great.

At the time of the writing of 1 Peter, the scattered, weak, and despised church of Christ needed to remember that the Lord was present with her. She was in need of a reminder that victory for her cause did not depend on wealth, power, or popularity – none of which she had – but on faithfulness to Christ. Discouragement is a subtle yet effective foe, and the Holy Spirit moved the apostle to bring a message of hope to these suffering people.

In the text for today's study, Christians are reminded that though the world may despise us, though we are pilgrims in a hostile land which is not our home, though we may have countless foes yet to face, we have a unique relationship with Christ which gives hope and courage.

29

We are "a chosen people, a royal priesthood, a holy nation, a people belonging to God." Because we are a specially honored people, we must live so as to "declare the praises of him who called you out of darkness into his wonderful light."

The knowledge that Christians are special people is not intended to produce pride but to give encouragement. When we consider the "painful trial" the original readers of Peter's epistles were facing, it is not difficult to understand why this theme was introduced. Beyond the need of those original readers, its present readers need the same message.

A Christian man became discouraged over some personal problems he was facing. He let them get the best of him. He left off prayer, turned away from the counsel of the Word of God, and became deeply entangled in sin. Few people cared enough to even try to reach him, and some of those who did try apparently used the wrong approach. But finally someone appealed for him to look at himself as God's child and to believe that he could overcome. His friend said, "You belong to the Lord. He has invested his love in you and washed you from sin by his blood. Now you have turned back from following him. How can you do it? You are special to God. He will help you put the pieces of your life together again. He will give you strength to handle your problems." The man accepted it. He had forgotten that he had a unique relationship with the Savior and needed to be reminded. He took courage and began to draw on the strength of God. Today he is useful again in the kingdom of heaven.

Do others of us need the same reminder?

Our Unique Relationship With Christ

At times religion has imposed barriers between men and the God we seek. Certainly the pagan religions, with their secretive priests and mystical ceremonies, did little to give the worshiper a sense of close communion with deity. Even the true God of heaven had to be approached for a time (i.e., under the Law of Moses) through the instrumentality of a "clergy" system. But the religion of Jesus Christ has made every worshiper a priest and is intended to make men feel a personal nearness to God.

As you come to him, the living Stone – rejected by men but chosen by God and precious to him – you also, like living stones, are being built into a spiritual house to be a holy priesthood, offering spiritual sacrifices acceptable to God through Jesus Christ (1 Pet. 2:4-5).

Christianity has occasionally been called a *priestless* religion. This text seems to refute such a notion. Christianity is a *priest-filled* religion. Every Christian is set apart to God from the rest of men for the sake of worship and service. Under the Old Testament system, only a few people were close enough to God to be his priests; today all of God's people are near to him because we are all *in Christ.*

Follow the argument carefully. Christ is elect and precious with God; all believers are in Christ and thus share in his honor; thus believers themselves are precious to God.

For in Scripture it says: "See, I lay a stone in Zion, a chosen and precious cornerstone, and the one who trusts in him will never be put to shame." Now to you who believe, this stone is precious. But to those who do not believe, "The stone the builders rejected has become the capstone," and, "A stone that causes men to stumble and a rock that makes them fall." They stumble because they disobey the message – which is also what they were destined for (1 Pet. 2:6-8).

The contrast between the two classes of men described here should not be overlooked. "Now to you who believe, this stone is precious." Since Christ is *the* cornerstone and each Christian is a living stone built upon him, every believer shares in his glory. But those who "stumble because they disobey the message" forfeit all hope of sharing his honor and preciousness before the Father. Christ challenges men and makes demands of us; the person who cannot submit to those challenges and demands is destined to stumble.

What a beautiful series of descriptive titles is used of those who belong to Christ.

> But you are a chosen people, a royal priesthood, a holy nation, a people belonging to God, that you may declare the praises of him who called you out of darkness into his wonderful light. Once you were not a people, but now you are the people of God; once you had not received mercy, but now you have received mercy (1 Pet. 2:9-10).

First, Christians are "a chosen people." The Hebrew race was once chosen and elect of God. But that race of men with fleshly ties through Abraham failed to respond to divine love and purpose as it should. So now heaven has selected a new race (or family) of men through whom to work in the world. The ties among the members of this race are spiritual rather than physical, and people of all earthly stocks may belong to this chosen family (cf. Rom. 2:28-29).

Second, the church is a "royal priesthood." Since Christ is now reigning over his kingdom (Acts 2:30-31), we are participating in that reign. Because of God's rich mercies, we have been made alive in Christ, raised with him, and "seated with him in the heavenly realms" (Eph. 2:4-6). It is a remarkable paradox, however, that this royal family does not sit in idleness but functions instead as a body of priests to serve the Living God. The apostle John made this same point when he wrote that Christ "has made us to be a kingdom and priests to serve his God and Father" (Rev. 1:6).

Third, Christians are a "holy nation." Recalling for a moment the concept of holiness studied in Chapter Three, this description designates the church as a separated people. God's people are not restricted to any one nation of the world by geographical boundaries. Instead, men of all nations, races, and classes are collectively considered a separated spiritual nation in Christ.

Fourth, Christians are a "people belonging to God." The older translation of this phrase to read "a peculiar people" (KJV) has proved most unfortunate. It misses the sense of the original text for the modern reader. The point is that God possesses, guards, and preserves for himself those people who are in his church. We belong to him in a way that other men do not, for we have been purchased by the blood of Christ (cf. Acts 20:28).

And why has God done all this? Why has he made us into a race, a priesthood, nation, and people of special possession? There is no creature in the universe who is so great and independent that he has been blessed of God for his personal benefit alone. Every man who receives something from the divine hand is thereby made a steward who is responsible for passing it on to others. Thus Peter affirms that Christians are to declare to the world, both by word and deed, the "praises" of God. This means that the love, wisdom, strength, and purity of God are to be seen through the lives of people who are saved. It is as if we were being told that we were not saved for our own sakes. Just as the heavens are a revelation to declare the power and glory of God (Psa. 19:1), so are faithful Christians a revelation of his personal attributes to mankind.

Christians are in a unique relationship with Christ. We no longer live in the darkness of ignorance and sin but in the light of his truth (Psa. 119:105, 130) and righteousness (1 John 1:7); we are his people, and we live through his mercy. Surely these facts are enough to convince us of the dignity and usefulness of the Christian life we are called to show the world.

Lest anyone should miss the implications of what has been said about the life Christians should be living, Peter traces those implications for three crucial areas of life. The relationship we have with Christ obligates us to fulfill some very special responsibilities to the world, to the state, and to masters.

Our Responsibility to the World

First, a Christian must keep himself free of entanglements with fleshly passions.

> Dear friends, I urge you, as aliens and strangers in the world, to abstain from sinful desires, which war against your soul. Live such good lives among the pagans that, though they accuse you of doing wrong, they may see your good deeds and glorify God on the day he visits us (1 Pet. 2:11-12).

Since the child of God is a citizen of heaven (Phil. 3:20), he should never allow himself to get tangled up in the things of the world. He is nothing more than a temporary resident. And if he should forget that fact and fall in love with the world, he could easily lose his soul. "Do not love the world or anything in the world. If anyone loves the world, the love of the Father is not in him" (1 John 2:15).

"Sinful desires" (fleshly lusts, ASV) are the base passions and evil desires which stand over against spiritual longings and the desire for righteousness. Such desires "war against your soul" and work to destroy purity and devotion to God.

Christians must also consider their influence upon people of the world who observe their behavior. Today we are familiar with what happens when a believer is unfaithful to his wife or steals money from his employer. Both he and all other believers in that community are held up to ridicule and called hypocrites. It seems to give worldly people a sense of relief to be able to point an accusing finger at one of us. This is all the more reason for every child of God to be scrupulously upright in all things and for churches to repudiate sin in their memberships by practicing consistent self-discipline (cf. 1 Cor. 5:1ff).

In the earliest days of the church, the situation was even worse than it is now. The Roman historian Tacitus called Christians "a class hated for their abominations," and evil rumors of all sorts circulated constantly about the disciples of Christ. They were accused of incest, cannibalism,

34

and many other hateful things. Thus they had to live down lies being told about them and overcome terrible prejudice. It is no wonder that Peter called for good works among his readers. His appeal in verse 12 reminds one of Jesus' words in the Sermon on the Mount: "Let your light shine before men, that they may see your good deeds and praise your Father in heaven" (Matt. 5:16).

Our Responsibility to the State

Second, a Christian must be a good citizen of the civil government to which he is subject.

> Submit yourselves for the Lord's sake to every authority instituted among men: whether to the king, as the supreme authority, or to governors, who are sent by him to punish those who do wrong and to commend those who do right. For it is God's will that by doing good you should silence the ignorant talk of foolish men. Live as free men, but do not use your freedom as a cover-up for evil; live as servants of God. Show proper respect to everyone: Love the brotherhood of believers, fear God, honor the king (1 Pet. 2:13-17).

One of the false charges made against Jesus was disloyalty to Rome. The Jews told Pilate, "He opposes payment of taxes to Caesar and claims to be Christ, a king" (Luke 23:2). The opposite was true, for Jesus taught his followers to show respect for Caesar and to pay their taxes (Matt. 22:21). The same charge of civil defiance was also lodged against Paul (Acts 24:5) and seems to have been used against Christians generally in the early days of the church.

Perhaps it was in response to these vicious rumors that the New Testament has so much to say about loyalty to civil governments. Paul made a major point of this in writing to believers in the capital city of the empire. "Everyone must submit himself to the governing authorities, for there is no authority except that which God has established. The authorities that exist have been established by God" (Rom. 13:1).

Only when the state makes a demand of its citizens that would require a Christian to defy God can he legitimately refuse to comply with civil law. Peter had been in such a situation at least once before at Jerusalem (cf. Acts 4:19-20), and this reservation is surely assumed in this text.

In being good citizens, followers of Christ silence the false and groundless criticisms of any who would charge them with disloyalty to the state.

We are no less obligated to heed this counsel today than our brothers were in the Roman Empire. Paying taxes, obeying speed laws, and fulfilling our other obligations to the state constitute a part of our duty to God.

Our Responsibility to Earthly Masters

Third, Peter called for Christians of his time to recognize their obligation to their masters. Many of the earliest converts to Christ were from the poorer people of the empire and were slaves. Because Christianity speaks of "freedom from bondage" and "equality," enemies of the faith circulated the rumor that its people were untrustworthy as slaves and likely to run away from or murder their masters. To counter this false report (and perhaps to prevent new converts from misunderstanding their spiritual "freedom" in Christ), both Peter and Paul had a great deal to say about slaves and their masters.

> Slaves, submit yourselves to your masters with all respect, not only to those who are good and considerate, but also to those who are harsh. For it is commendable if a man bears up under the pain of unjust suffering because he is conscious of God. But how is it to your credit if you receive a beating for doing wrong and endure it? But if you suffer for doing good and you endure it, this is commendable before God. To this you were called, because Christ suffered for you, leaving you an example, that you should follow in his steps. "He committed no sin, and no deceit was found in his mouth." When they hurled their insults at him, he did not retaliate; when he suffered, he

made no threats. Instead, he entrusted himself to him who judges justly. He himself bore our sins in his body on the tree, so that we might die to sins and live for righteousness; by his wounds you have been healed. For you were like sheep going astray, but now you have returned to the Shepherd and Overseer of your souls (1 Pet. 2:18-25).

The Christian religion is inimical to slavery, and its doctrines of love and respect for one's fellows ultimately destroyed the institution in places where its teachings were believed and conscientiously applied (cf. Phile. 16). But so long as the institution did exist, Christians who were unfortunate enough to be slaves were told to use their role as an opportunity to prove that Christianity was no threat to order. After all, the religion of Jesus Christ is not primarily concerned with the existing social and cultural patterns of people as it is concerned with their spiritual deliverance from sin.

If a slave happened to belong to a decent man, his lot in life might be easier to bear than one whose master was cruel and inhumane. Yet it was in the latter situation rather than the former that a Christian could show his faith more effectively. Christ suffered injustice and endured it for the sake of a higher good. Sometimes it will be necessary for his followers to do the same. Without legal redress for some grievance (e.g., Paul's unjust arrests and treatment in Acts), one may have to endure with great self-restraint and show himself capable of bearing reproach in the way his Master did.

Paul gives very similar counsel to this in Ephesians 6:5-8. He told slaves to sanctify their unpleasant tasks by serving as unto the Lord rather than to mere men. This would allow them to turn what otherwise might be a humiliating task that would generate hatred into a work done in Christ's name and to his praise.

Do these principles governing slave-master relationships have any value for people who do not live with the awful institution of slavery? The Christian in school who has a teacher who makes what the student considers unreasonable assignments and grades exams unfairly is being put to the test. He can complain and grumble to no profit, or he can perform to the best of his ability so as to show the spirit of Christ. The man whose employer is inconsiderate and never shows appreciation for the work done for him is in a situation of special opportunity. By suffering in the context of work properly done and taking it patiently, he pleases the Lord. He walks away from the completed task not with seething anger but with a sense of spiritual accomplishment. Christianity challenges the best that is in us.

Conclusion

We sometimes forget that the world generally will never appreciate and applaud faithful Christians. They will misinterpret our meekness as weakness; they will see our submission to distasteful authority as cowardice; they will view our separation from fleshly lusts as some sort of self-righteous fanaticism. Unless we understand that it is God's praise rather than man's we are seeking, we will be turned aside by discouragment from the divine will for our lives.

We are Christ's people. We belong to him and our citizenship is above. When our commitment to him calls for sacrifices to be made or for hardships to be endured, the knowledge that we are his special people gives us *something to hold on to*.

Chapter Five

Wives and Husbands

1 Peter 3:1-7

The covenant relationship of marriage owes its origin to the purposive will of Almighty God. For the benefit of man and woman, this relationship was established in Eden.

> The Lord God said, "It is not good for the man to be alone. I will make a helper suitable for him."
> ... So the Lord God caused the man to fall into a deep sleep; and while he was sleeping, he took one of the man's ribs and closed up the place with flesh. Then the Lord God made a woman from the rib he had taken out of the man, and he brought her to the man. ... For this reason a man will leave his father and mother and be united to his wife, and they will become one flesh (Gen. 2:18, 21-22, 24).

During the interval of time between the origination of marriage in Eden and the coming of Jesus into the world, this holy institution suffered many abuses. In the Jewish world, wives were typically regarded as possessions. It was unthinkable for a wife to leave her husband, although her husband could divorce her at any time for the most trivial of causes. In the Gentile world, the situation was even more cruel. A woman had no rights or protection under law, and she was completely at the mercy of her husband. He literally had the power of life and death over her. The Roman writer Cato reflects the situation when he says: "If your were to catch your wife in the act of infidelity, you can kill her with impunity without a trial; but, if she were to catch you, she would not venture to touch you with her finger, and, indeed, she has no right."

It was the coming of Christianity which changed all this. The religion of Jesus Christ restored marriage to what it was at the first. It gave an even deeper and holier meaning to marriage by using this relationship as an image of the union between Christ and the church (cf. Eph. 5:22ff). Christianity has caused us to change our concept of a husband from that of a ruling tyrant to one of a self-sacrificing man who puts the welfare of his wife above his own. It has changed our concept of a wife from that of a mistress and child-bearer to one of a partner who shares everything which is her husband's life. The love, kindness, and peace which we associate with a Christian home were not the notions of "home" in men's minds before the advent of Christianity.

In studying the verses which constitute the text for this study, we shall be reading lines which surely must have shocked many of the first-century people who originally read them.

A Silent Sermon

Ironically, the Christian religion introduced an element of sharp division into many families when it was first preached. There would be occasional situations where one member of a family unit would receive Christ and thereby be set against parent, companion, or child. Jesus warned that this would occur, and he acknowledged that such people would have to make a heart-rending choice as to their loyalty. He said that his presence in the world would put some men at odds with their fathers, some daughers with their mothers, daughters-in-law with mothers-in-law, etc. He said: "Anyone who loves his father or mother more than me is not worthy of me; and anyone who loves his son or daughter more than me is not worthy of me" (Matt. 10:34-37).

I have known a few people in my lifetime who had to choose between Christ and their families. A godly elder once told me – with tears coursing down his cheeks – about the decision he had made over fifty years before to become a Christian. His family never again treated him as anything more than a stranger. A young man of recent acquaintance was disowned by his family for becoming a Christian, and his father rewrote his will to guarantee that none of his considerable estate should ever go to him and be used on behalf of the gospel.

Such situations in the first-century world would have been even more extreme than today, especially for a woman. Women of that time had few rights, and they dared not make any decision of consequence independently of their husbands. What must have been the problems of a wife who became a Christian in the time of the apostles! If her husband was still a Jew or a worshiper of pagan deities, what abuse she would have had to bear. It would be next to impossible for us to appreciate all that would have been involved.

If a man became a Christian but his wife did not, she could do nothing about it. But if a woman became a Christian and her husband did not, he could do plenty to make her life miserable. It is because the woman was so much more vulnerable in a divided home that Peter devoted quite a bit more space to advising wives than husbands in our text. As we study this material, it should (1) make all of us more sympathetic to those Christians we know today who live with unbelieving companions, (2) give guidance to those who are in such a situation, and (3) warn young people against marrying outside the faith.

Here is inspired counsel to the woman who is married to someone who is not a Christian:

Wives, in the same way be submissive to your husbands so that, if any of them do not believe the word, they may be won over without talk by the behavior of their wives, when they see the purity and reverence of your lives (1 Pet. 3:1-2).

Notice the counsel *not* given. The wife is not advised to leave her husband under these circumstances, for she is the Lord's best hope of reaching him with the gospel. She is not told to argue and nag, for that would have the opposite effect from what Peter would like to see happen. She is not told to take authority over her husband to instruct him formally in the new faith she has embraced, for Christianity forbids the woman to assume such a role in relation to men (cf. 1 Tim. 2:12).

In this connection, it is interesting to notice the counsel given the same class of women through Paul.

And if a woman has a husband who is not a believer and he is willing to live with her, she must not divorce him. For the unbelieving husband has been sanctified through his wife, and the unbelieving wife has been sanctified through her believing husband. Otherwise your children would be unclean, but as it is, they are holy.

But if the unbeliever leaves, let him do so. A believing man or woman is not bound in such circumstances; God has called us to live in peace. How do you know, wife, whether you will save your husband? Or, how do you know, husband, whether you will save your wife? (1 Cor. 7:13-16).

Don't leave your unbelieving husband, for both he and your children are "sanctified" and "holy" (note: both words mean "set apart") by your presence. That is, the Christian member of the family is regarded as the firstfruits of the family unto the Lord, and the remaining members of the group were viewed as "set apart" unto the Lord (i.e., as prospects for conversion) through the Christian's influence.

What, then, is Peter's counsel to these wives? How can they save their beloved mates and children?

First, "be submissive to your husbands." It would be a travesty against Christ for a woman to use her faith as an excuse for pride and thus hold her unbelieving husband in contempt. She should rather see the need for being a better wife than she has ever been before. Let her submit to him lovingly and selflessly so as to make him kindly disposed to the religion which would teach her such virtue. It is not difficult to understand how this would go far in breaking down the barriers of prejudice and hostility.

Second, let her exhibit "purity" in her behavior. Let her life be pure and above reproach, both in relation to her husband and to everyone else.

Third, let her behavior exhibit proper "reverence" toward her husband. She should carefully avoid giving any unnecessary offense. She should not press the differences which were separating her from her husband so as to drive the wedge deeper.

The wife who is a Christian will not have to go out of her way to create friction with her non-Christian husband. The problems will be there. And the silent eloquence of a godly life will be more powerful for her case than argument and controversy. As one writer has expressed it: "Her only weapon must be the silent preaching of a lovely life."

A Beautiful Wife

Peter goes on to describe the woman who is truly beautiful. She is the Christian woman who devotes her efforts to spiritual adornment.

> Your beauty should not come from outward adornment, such as braided hair and the wearing of gold jewelry and fine clothes. Instead, it should be that of your inner self, the unfading beauty of a gentle and quiet spirit, which is of great worth in God's sight (1 Pet. 3:3-4).

This passage does not forbid a godly woman to give attention to her physical appearance. In fact, she would reflect dishonor upon her Lord if she were to be careless in this regard. What the text does forbid is dressing in such a way as to be showy and to draw attention to herself. And just as surely as one can violate this injunction by wearing garish clothes and outlandish hairdos, she can also draw attention to herself by going to the opposite extreme. There is an obvious pitfall here into which certain radical sects have fallen by forcing their women to wear the styles of a century ago. There is no surer way to draw attention to a woman than by having her walk the streets in that kind of garb, yet the people who practice this believe themselves to be obeying 1 Peter 3:3.

A Christian woman is not forbidden all braiding of the hair or wearing of gold any more than the wearing of clothes. She is reminded, however, that these things which adorn the outer person are worthless when compared to the valuable traits about to be mentioned – "the unfading beauty of a gentle and quiet spirit." It is a matter of relative value. The former are not sinful when in good taste and not to parade one's vanity; the latter are of infinite worth and serve to keep the other in perspective. As one writer has put it: "The world admires rich dress and covets costly jewels; God applauds the meek and quiet spirit. Which of the two should the Christian seek to please – God or the world?"

The woman who makes herself beautiful to her husband by developing "a gentle and quiet spirit" will have become God's instrument to bless that man. She will have proved her love for him in the most meaningful way possible.

In this connection and in order to reinforce the point being made, Peter recalls the godly women of the Old Testament era:

> For this is the way the holy women of the past who put their hope in God used to make themselves beautiful. They were submissive to their own husbands, like Sarah, who obeyed Abraham and called him her master. You are her daughters if you do what is right and do not give way to fear (1 Pet. 3:5-6).

These holy women of old are examples to Christian women. They placed their emphasis not on things of the flesh but on things of the spirit. In particular, as exemplified by Sarah, they recognized and submitted to the authority of their husbands.

In the twentieth century, this counsel sounds quite out of place to most people. Materialism encourages everyone to judge success and beauty in terms of display and wealth. And feminist movements have gained such momentum that many women now resent their "traditional" role in society and have made it clear that they do not intend to "be in subjection" to their husbands.

A Considerate Husband

In all fairness, however, it may be the case that the modern feminist movements have been spawned by men who misused their positions of authority and leadership. After all, the Bible does not give husbands the right to be tyrants. Some women may have been driven to resentment by demanding, inconsiderate, and abusive men.

Having spoken of the duties of wives to their husbands, Peter acknowledges the mutual obligations of marriage by his counsel to men.

> Husbands, in the same way be considerate as you live with your wives, and treat them with respect as the weaker partner and as heirs with you of the gracious gift of life, so that nothing will hinder your prayers (1 Pet. 3:7).

Both husband and wife are "partners" in an arrangement created for the glory of God (cf. Rom. 9:21-23). The woman is the "weaker partner" only with regard to her general physical strength; she is not intellectually or spiritually inferior to the man (cf. Gal. 3:28). Accounting her to be precious and realizing that he is obligated to protect and care for her, the Christian husband is to treat his wife with special respect and consideration. Just as Christ never acted in an unloving manner toward his bride (i.e., the church), so must the Christian husband guard his conduct toward his wife. "Husbands, love your wives, just as Christ loved the church and gave himself up for her ..." (Eph. 5:25).

If a marriage is the spiritual relationship God wants it to be, the partners see themselves as heirs of God (joint-heirs of the grace of life, ASV) and make every effort to aid each other in attaining the goal of eternal fellowship with the Father, Son, and Holy Spirit.

Finally, Peter reminds the Christian husband that he will "hinder" his attempts at prayer if he neglects to show the loving and considerate attention to his wife's needs that heaven expects him to demonstrate. What a thought this is for every male member of the body of Christ to keep in mind.

Conclusion

Christianity changed the way people viewed the marriage and family relationship. And in those situations of special challenge where a Christian was alone in his or her devotion to Christ within the family unit, there was seen a unique opportunity for that person to glorify God and serve the other family members.

The home is under heavy pressures again today. As in the first century, some homes are divided. Many more have no spiritual allegiance whatever. Husbands are inconsiderate, and wives resist giving their mates the leadership role God has ordained for them. How we need to get back to God's plan for husband-wife relationships. Then our homes would have *something to hold on to.*

Chapter Six

Suffering for Doing Right

1 Peter 3:8-22

Both 1 and 2 Peter were written on the eve of a severe persecution of the church in and around Rome. The source of this attack on the people of God was the infamous Nero.

Nero came to the Roman emperorship in A.D. 54 when his mother poisoned his adoptive father, Claudius, and ruled until his death by suicide in A.D. 68. During his reign he murdered several members of his family and made countless enemies. When a great fire broke out in the capital city during July of A.D. 64, the citizenry suspected the emperor himself of having started it, and a rumor to that effect was circulated widely. The Roman historian, Tacitus, relates how Nero attempted to shift suspicion from himself.

> Consequently, to get rid of the report, Nero fastened the guilt and inflicted the most exquisite tortures on a class hated for their abominations, called Christians by the populace. ... Mockery of every sort was added to their deaths. Covered with the skins of beasts, they were torn by dogs and perished, or were nailed

47

to crosses, or were doomed to flames and burned, to serve as a nightly illumination when daylight had expired. Nero offered his gardens for the spectacle, and was exhibiting a show in the circus, while he mingled with the people in the dress of a charioteer or stood aloft on a car (*Annals* 15.44.).

Tradition has it that both Peter and Paul died in the persecution under Nero, the former by crucifixion and the latter by beheading.

The Lord warned his disciples that many of them would suffer persecution for his sake. The final Beatitude pronounced a blessing on "those who are persecuted because of righteousness." In the same context, Jesus reminded his disciples that the prophets of old had suffered for their faith in exactly this manner (Matt. 5:11-12).

Jesus specifically told Peter that he would die as a martyr for the faith. Prior to his ascension to the Father and in the setting of having just reassured the fisherman-apostle of his usefulness to the kingdom of God, he warned Peter that in his later years he would be at the mercy of others. John, commenting on Jesus' words, wrote: "Jesus said this to indicate the kind of death by which Peter would glorify God" (John 21:18-19a).

It is an age-old problem that is raised here: Why do good men suffer for their righteousness while the wicked seem to prosper?

Suffering for doing right is spoken of frequently in the Word of God. Paul said, "Everyone who wants to live a godly life in Christ Jesus will be persecuted" (2 Tim. 3:12). Jesus told the apostles, "Remember the words I spoke to you: 'No servant is greater than his master.' If they persecuted me, they will persecute you also" (John 15:20).

In the section of text to be studied in this lesson, we hear Peter warning his readers that many of them will have to share in suffering soon. His tone is not morbid, however. He was simply trying to prepare his readers – as well as himself – for what lay ahead. Doubtless many of the people who read the original epistle later laid down their lives for the faith.

Preparing for the Onslaught

Before a team goes onto the field for some athletic contest, the team members need to get their signals straight. They must know their fellow participants and be ready to work with them unselfishly for the sake of the contest. In a similar way, Peter spoke first about the relationship which needed to exist among the Christians before they entered the great struggle with Nero.

> Finally, all of you, live in harmony with one another; be sympathetic, love as brothers, be compassionate and humble. Do not repay evil with evil or insult with insult, but with blessing, because to this you were called so that you may inherit a blessing (1 Pet. 3:8-9).

First, they needed to be *united and living in harmony.* In some situations, unity is viewed as "good" or "desirable"; in others it is absolutely necessary. One of those times when God's people must stand together is when they are being confronted by a strong and determined foe.

There is something about danger that causes men to forget their petty differences for the sake of safety. From history we observe this principle with men and nations. In times of peace, dissident elements within a society may turn on one another; when faced with a common foe, they stand shoulder to shoulder. The first-century church had a sense of unity and fellowship due to some degree to the persecution against her from first the Jews and later the Romans. We seem to lack that close bond today, and Satan is weakening us through division. Maybe we need a dose of hardship to help us unite for the sake of strength and power. "If you keep on biting and devouring each other, watch out or you will be destroyed by each other" (Gal. 5:15). "I appeal to you, brothers, in the name of our Lord Jesus Christ, that all of you agree with one another so that there may be no divisions among you ..." (1 Cor. 1:10).

Second, they needed to be *sympathetic.* Sympathy is the ability to step outside one's own concerns in order to identify with and share the pains of another. It is an act of love and selflessness. When all the Christians were suffering persecution under Nero, there would be a temptation for each to be so preoccupied with his own peril that he would neglect looking out for someone else and his needs.

In the selfish atmosphere in which we live now, Christians are tempted to ignore each other, to isolate ourselves from each other. We need to work at "being like-minded, having the same love, being one in spirit and purpose"; we need to be able to look beyond our own interests to the concerns and needs of others (Phil. 2:2-4). We are interdependent members of Christ's body: "If one part suffers, every part suffers with it; if one part is honored, every part rejoices with it" (1 Cor. 12:26).

Third, they needed to *"love as brothers."* Born again into the family of God, every believer is expected to have a special relationship with every other. "A new command I give you: Love one another. As I have loved you, so you must love one another. By this all men will know that you are my disciples, if you love one another" (John 13:34-35).

As the suffering saints of early centuries shared their goods with each other and proved themselves willing to die for one another, a profound impact was made on unbelievers. Tertullian wrote (ca. A.D. 200):

> But it is mainly the deeds of a love so noble that lead many to put a brand upon us. 'See,' they say 'how they love one another,' for they themselves are animated by mutual hatred; 'see how they are ready even to die for one another,' for they themselves will rather put to death (*Apology 39*).

Fourth, they needed to be *compassionate*. The heart of compassion is one able to be touched by the needs of people around him; it is able to care about another's plight; it is sensitive to the fact that others are carrying terrible burdens. "Be kind and compassionate to one another, forgiving each other, just as in Christ God forgave you" (Eph. 4:32).

Many writers and poets have called attention to the lack

of such a spirit as this in our modern world. We watch the evening news on TV and see color photos of starving children, bombed villages, bleeding accident victims, and bodies smashed by earthquakes. We sigh and change the channel to watch our favorite program. We seem to forget that these scenes are of real people, that their tragedy has left a trail of broken hearts. Christians must be Christ-like in our ability to be touched by such things.

Fifth, they needed to be *humble.* Humility grows out of one's sense of dependence upon God. The Christian is not self-sufficient; his sufficiency is in Christ. In speaking of his ministry, Paul said, "Not that we are competent in ourselves to claim anything for ourselves, but our competence comes from God" (2 Cor. 3:5). There is no room for personal pride and haughtiness in a child of God. The experiences of testing about to be faced by Peter's original readers would reinforce this truth to them.

Sixth, they needed to be *forgiving.* When someone is suffering at the hands of another, the natural tendency is to strike back; if weakness keeps him from striking back, he can at least show his hatred and defiance. Christians must not yield to this inclination. Christ taught us to love and pray for our enemies (Matt. 5:44) and set us an example in praying for his own murderers (Luke 23:34). Paul used language very similar to that of our text when he wrote: "Do not repay anyone evil for evil. ... On the contrary, 'If your enemy is hungry, feed him; if he is thirsty, give him something to drink ...' Do not be overcome by evil, but overcome evil with good" (Rom. 12:17-21).

Only with these traits of spirit can Christians face, overcome, and derive spiritual blessing from their trials.

For, "Whoever would love life and see good days must keep his tongue from evil and his lips from deceitful speech. He must turn from evil and do good; he must seek peace and pursue it. For the eyes of the Lord are on the righteous and his ears are attentive to their prayer, but the face of the Lord is against those who do evil" (1 Pet. 3:10-12).

Zealous for the Good

The mother of a four-year-old girl died, and a friend of the family was holding and trying to comfort her. With his own heart aching, the man wondered aloud, "Darling, what will you do now?" The little girl replied, "I guess I'll just keep on going to Sunday School." Her answer was the correct one to give. When trials and heartaches come, the thing to do is not to withdraw from the world but to keep on doing the will of God. This was Peter's counsel to his readers:

> Who is going to harm you if you are eager to do good? But even if you should suffer for what is right, you are blessed. "Do not fear what they fear; do not be frightened." But in your hearts set apart Christ as Lord. Always be prepared to give an answer to everyone who asks you to give the reason for the hope that you have. But do this with gentleness and respect, keeping a clear conscience, so that those who speak maliciously against your good behavior in Christ may be ashamed of their slander. It is better, if it is God's will, to suffer for doing good than for doing evil (1 Pet. 3:13-17).

When you are threatened, do not give way to fear; God is with you. When you are arrested and brought before your persecutors, be ready to present a reasoned defense of your faith; your cause is true. When your enemies slander you, let your conscience be clear because of your righteousness; your lives are lived in imitation of Christ.

This is a call for boldness. Yet his readers knew that Peter was demanding nothing of them which he had not already demonstrated in his own life. Luke tells us of an episode involving the Sanhedrin at Jerusalem: "When they saw the courage (boldness, ASV) of Peter and John and realized that they were unschooled, ordinary men, they were astonished and they took note that these men had been with Jesus" (Acts 4:13). This is a model for all Christians in similar situations. Confess your faith boldly; give the reasons for your hope in Christ; allow your enemies to see Christ in your behavior.

The Example of Christ

Yet it was not his own experience that Peter put forth as an example for his readers. He pointed to the ideal example of Christ.

> For Christ died for sins once for all, the righteous for the unrighteous, to bring you to God. He was put to death in the body but made alive by the Spirit, through whom also he went and preached to the spirits in prison who disobeyed long ago when God waited patiently in the days of Noah while the ark was being built. In it only a few people, eight in all, were saved through water, and this water symbolizes baptism that now saves you also – not the removal of dirt from the body but the pledge of a good conscience toward God. It saves you by the resurrection of Jesus Christ, who has gone into heaven and is at God's right hand – with angels, authorities and powers in submission to him (1 Pet. 3:18-22).

When a Christian of any period in history is called on to suffer for doing right, he should remember how much the Savior suffered for him. Furthermore, he should remember that Christ did not weaken and sin during his suffering. This epistle has already reminded us that "Christ suffered for you, leaving you an example, that ye should follow in his steps." Specifically, "When they hurled their insults at him, he did not retaliate; when he suffered, he made no threats. Instead, he entrusted himself to him who judges justly" (1 Pet. 2:21-23). This is our perfect example of suffering.

Having introduced the sufferings of Christ, Peter writes a very beautiful summary of salvation in verses 18-22. Jesus died for our sins and was raised for our justification (v. 18; cf. Rom. 4:25); we receive salvation when we are buried with him in baptism (v. 21; cf. Rom. 6:3-4); we are members of his kingdom, the church, and are subject to his authority (v. 22; cf. Acts 2:32-36).

Conclusion

Suffering for doing right is not a new thing.

> And what more shall I say? I do not have time to tell about Gideon, Barak, Samson, Jephthah, David, Samuel and the prophets, who through faith conquered kingdoms, administered justice, and gained what was promised; who shut the mouths of lions, quenched the fury of the flames, and escaped the edge of the sword; whose weakness was turned to strength; and who became powerful in battle and routed foreign armies. Women received back their dead, raised to life again. Others were tortured and refused to be released, so that they might obtain a better resurrection. Some faced jeers and flogging, while still others were chained and put in prison. They were stoned; they were sawed in two; they were put to death by the sword. They went about in sheepskins and goatskins, destitute, persecuted and mistreated – the world was not worthy of them (Heb. 11:32-38).

The willingness to endure suffering for the sake of Christ and to return good for evil has proved to be one of the most appealing features of our religion. In one of the many terrible and savage wars which have been fought in the Middle East, a young woman and her brother were chased down a street by an enemy soldier and into a blind alley. There the girl's brother was slain before her eyes. She leaped over a wall and escaped. Later she was working as a nurse in a military hospital when the man who murdered her brother was brought into her ward. He was now a prisoner, wounded and very ill; it would take only a bit of neglect to insure his death. The young woman later, when safe in America, confessed to the struggle that went on in her heart. One part of her cried, "Vengeance." What she knew of Christ cried, "Love." To the good of both patient and nurse, she cared for him as patiently and tenderly as for anyone in her ward. When the recovering soldier recognized the woman and was unable to conceal his curiosity any longer, he asked his nurse why she had not let him die. She said, "I am a follower of him who commanded his people to love their enemies and do them good." The man was silent for a long while. At last he spoke: "I never knew there was such a religion. Tell me more about it, please, for I want it for myself."

Christians can endure suffering for the sake of righteousness, for we have *something to hold on to.*

Chapter Seven

An Attitude Toward Life

1 Peter 4:1-11

What is the meaning of human life? How does one find purpose for his existence? By what standard (if any) should one measure his behavior? Should each man look only for personal happiness, or should he seek the interests of others? Will there be any final reckoning to be made of one's life?

The questions above are terribly old and common. Socrates sought to define the upright life, and philosophers since his time have wrestled with the same issue.

The fact remains, however, that these old and common questions are still the most vital and personal questions any person can raise. Books and magazine articles come from the presses daily to sell some philosophy of life. TV and radio talk shows raise these problems with celebrity guests and audience participants. And when a man is sobered by the death of someone close to him or the doctor's finding that he has a terminal disease, these are the issues above all others in importance to him.

Biblical theism is one attitude toward life and its meaning. This view holds that man is created by God, uniquely loved by him, and a candidate for eternal fellowship with him. This view entails the recognition by man of his responsibility to seek after God and do his will.

Naturalism is an opposite view of man's existence and nature. It sees man merely as a product of nature, a high-level animal whose unique endowments are the chance outworkings of a blind evolutionary process. Life is not "going" anywhere according to this philosophy, except to the grave. Therefore some degree of personal happiness (whatever he conceives that to be) is all the individual can hope to achieve.

Between the poles of biblical theism and naturalism, a variety of other answers to the questions raised earlier have been offered.

The purpose of this lesson is not to list and evaluate these alternate philosophies of life. It is to see how biblical theism translates into life. The verses we shall study from the pen of the apostle Peter are the inspired guidelines for daily living to be followed by one who holds that his life belongs to God.

Our age has been called The Confused Generation. We have so much to live *with* but so little to live *for*. Even some Christians fit this mold. They admit that their lives lack direction and purpose. It is not the will of God that his people should live in such bewilderment.

First Peter 4:1-11 suggests three very practical guidelines for the life of a Christian. It would not be incorrect to say that these verses state the practical outcome of a Christian philosophy of life.

Living in Purity

First, the child of God repudiates the lusts of the flesh and commits himself to follow the will of God by living a pure life.

> Therefore, since Christ suffered in his body, arm yourselves also with the same attitude, because he who has suffered in his body is done with sin. As a result, he does not live the rest of his earthly life for

evil human desires, but rather for the will of God (1 Pet. 4:1-2).

The saints of Peter's time were facing severe trials for the sake of their faith. They would have to be very sure of their motives and commitment from the beginning. They would need to have the same pure motive that gave Christ his strength to face and conquer sufferings. He was able to say, "My food is to do the will of him who sent me and to finish his work" (John 4:34). Only if Christians can say the same thing will they be safe in similar circumstances.

Before one becomes a Christian, such a view of life is impossible. Living for self is the accepted pattern of behavior. Finding a new thrill which will surpass yesterday's excitement is the goal of each day. The inability to possess all that can be desired is a constant source of anxiety.

It is most difficult for the modern reader to realize that the pagan world of apostolic days was far more lustful, immoral, and base than our own time. Only the days of Noah might have been worse than the Roman world of the first century. Therefore we likely cannot appreciate the force of the language when Peter writes:

> For you have spent enough time in the past doing what pagans choose to do – living in debauchery, lust, drunkenness, orgies, carousing and detestable idolatry. They think it strange that you do not plunge with them into the same flood of dissipation, and they heap abuse on you (1 Pet. 4:3-5).

After using several words which describe specific sins (i.e., debauchery, lust, drunkenness, etc.), Peter uses a broad term (Gk., *asotia*) to characterize the life of indulgence which the pagans characteristically sought. The KJV and ASV translate the word "riot," but our present use of that word to describe mob violence or civil unrest is not a correct representation of the Greek word used by the apostle. The NIV is better with its use of "dissipation" or the RSV with "profligacy," terms which suggest moral abandon.

Asotia (cf. Eph. 5:18; Tit. 1:16) signifies a reckless life which has abandoned all self-control. It describes someone like the Prodigal Son whose undisciplined behavior in the "far country" had no regard for God or decent people.

The Christians, of course, gave up this sort of life upon their conversion. The unconverted people who observed this change in their behavior thought it "strange" that anyone would give up such pleasures. Beyond that, they turned on the Christians in resentment and were heaping abuse on them. From non-biblical sources, we know that the Romans regarded Christian morality as a repressive system and called its teachers and practitioners "haters of mankind." Such people will answer to Christ in the Day of Judgment for their cruel reproaches of godly people.

Christianity demands a life of purity from its adherents. There is no way to follow Christ and live a reckless life of moral irresponsibility, for Christ and sin are eternally incompatible. As Paul expressed it, Christians are obliged to "behave decently" and "clothe yourselves with the Lord Jesus Christ"; once this has been done, the born-again soul will "not think about how to gratify the desires of the sinful nature" (Rom. 13:13-14).

Living With the End in View

Second, the Christian keeps in mind that he will answer to God for the life he lives on earth.

> But they will have to give account to him who is ready to judge the living and the dead. For this is the reason the gospel was preached even to those who are now dead, so that they might be judged according to men in regard to the body, but live according to God in regard to the spirit.
>
> The end of all things is near. Therefore be clear minded and self-controlled so that you can pray (1 Pet. 4:5-7).

It is interesting that this text views preparedness for Judgment as the purpose which prompted the preaching of the gospel. Judaism and Christianity view history as linear, i.e., going somewhere, purposive. Other religions view history as circular, going nowhere, without meaning. Where is history going? To Judgment! God has "set a day when he will judge the world with justice by the man he has appointed" (Acts 17:31).

Some have tried to link the preaching of the gospel "to those who are now dead" in verse six to what is referred to in 3:1-9. By this they seek to establish a situation in which the offer of salvation can somehow be made to men in the world of departed spirits (i.e., Hades). Such a doctrine would be inconsistent with all the New Testament has to say about salvation and personal responsibility in this life. It would falsify the appeal that "now is the day of salvation" (cf. 2 Cor. 6:2) and set up the possibility of a man defying God for a lifetime only to be saved by the offer of pardon in another world. The Bible clearly teaches that death seals one's eternal destiny and that no one will pass from one state to another in Hades (cf. Luke 16:19-31).

Although it is admitted that this part of the passage is difficult, it seems best to view the dead persons in view as deceased Christians. They had the gospel preached to them while they were alive; they lived faithful lives before their God and now are dead; and although sinful men may judge them fools for refusing wicked pleasures and going to their graves despised, God will reward them with eternal life.

Perhaps a greater problem in this passage is Peter's reference to the end of all things being "near" or "at hand" (ASV). Was he speaking of the Judgment? If so, how could it have been "near" two thousand years ago? Raymond Kelcy has responded to these questions by writing:

In view of the fact that Christ had said, 'but of that day and hour no one knows, not even the angels of heaven, nor the Son, but the Father only' (Matt. 24:36), it may be asked how Peter could affirm that the time has come near. In reply it might be said that Jesus had spoken of the destruction of Jerusalem and had given certain precursory signs by which it could be known that that terrible event was near (Matt. 24:3-35). But when he came to speak of the day of his second coming, he gave no precursory signs. He told the disciples that the event will be unexpected and that they must be constantly watchful and ready (Matt. 24:42-44). He seems to give emphasis to the fact that, after the destruction of Jerusalem, the next great event to look for is the end of the world. This means that for the people of God the second coming of Christ is an event that has constantly been suspended, and, so far as they know, is likely to occur at any time. In the sense, then, that *the end of all things* is an impending event, Peter may speak of it as that which is *at hand.* (*The Letters of Peter and Jude*, pp. 87-88).

Perhaps at no point are modern Christians more unlike first-century Christians than with regard to our attitude toward the second coming of Christ. "The Lord's coming is near" (Jas. 5:8b). "The Lord is near" (Phil. 4:5).

Whether reading the New Testament or viewing our present situation before the Lord, let us not confuse *immediacy* with *imminence.* Neither Peter nor today's saint could legitimately argue for the immediate return of Christ, for no man can know the day or hour of his coming (Mark 13:32). But both can hold that his parousia and the Judgment are imminent in that they could occur at any moment.

This is part of the Christian's perspective on life and is one reason why he lives as he does. He cannot be unconcerned about today, for he expects to give account of its use at the end of the way. Keeping this in view helps him to live as he ought to live.

Living for Others

Third, the child of God lives unselfishly, concerned not merely about himself but others as well. "Above all, love each other deeply, because love covers over a multitude of sins" (1 Pet. 4:8).

Exhortations to love among the people of God are frequent in Scripture. "And over all these virtues put on love, which binds them all together in perfect unity" (Col. 3:14). "Dear friends, let us love one another, for love comes from God. Everyone who loves has been born of God and knows God" (1 John 4:7). Of particular interest from our text is the observation that love among Christians "covers over a multitude of sins."

How does love *cover* sins? The child of God who loves his brother or sister as he should does not take offense easily. He bears with weaknesses and faults. He does not store up grievances and look for an opportunity to get even. He does not tell others the unfavorable things he knows about someone. To the contrary, he looks for ways to help the person. He seeks to restore the erring (cf. Gal. 6:1). He tries to encourage the weak. He helps to incorporate the Christian whose personality tends to keep him aloof and uninvolved into the fellowship of believers.

Love also causes Christians to "Offer hospitality to one another without grumbling" (1 Pet. 4:9). Travel in the first-century world was not the convenient thing it is today. Inns were not common, and the ones which existed had bad reputations. Christians moving from place to place therefore needed access to one another's homes. Today our need is not so much for this specific act of service as it is for Christians to open their hearts and homes to one another in hospitality of a general nature. Members sometimes complain about "cold churches." Perhaps they should help solve the problem by making it a point to get to know their brothers and sisters through personal contact. Take the initiative and ask a new couple over to your house. Have one or more of the elders and their wives to dinner. Promote activities which will get young people together with other young Christians.

Hospitality requires that one go to some trouble and expense. It ties up time, and most of us feel that we do not have any to spare. But Christian love causes us to make the effort without complaint.

Whatever the child of God has should be viewed as a means to service for the sake of others.

> Each one should use whatever gift he has received to serve others, faithfully administering God's grace in its various forms (1 Pet. 4:10).

The word "gift" here has been the object of some discussion. Does it refer to miraculous gifts possessed by a few in the early church? Or does it refer to the natural endowments possessed by Christians of every age? The principle is the same in either case, and the application to a modern reader is identical. We must use whatever possessions and abilities we have for the good of the whole body, the church.

> If anyone speaks, he should do it as one speaking the very words of God. If anyone serves, he should do it with the strength God provides, so that in all things God may be praised through Jesus Christ. To him be the glory and the power for ever and ever. Amen (1 Pet. 4:11).

God is glorified through the Son whenever Christians use their gifts wisely.

Conclusion

We sometimes complain that life is so complex and challenging one can never know just what to do. Are we not deceiving ourselves? Do we think that such a view excuses us when we fail? From a divine point of view, human life is just this simple: "Fear God and keep his commandments, for this is the whole duty of man" (Eccl. 12:13).

When one has a Christian perspective on life and its management, he has *something to hold on to*.

Chapter Eight

Wearing the Name "Christian"

1 Peter 4:12-19

The ministry of Jesus among sinful men brought great suffering to him. As had been foretold by Isaiah, the Christ was "despised and rejected of men"; he was "a man of sorrows and acquainted with grief" (cf. Isa. 53:1-3). He made this prediction of his own fate to the apostles: "[The Son of Man] will be handed over to the Gentiles. They will mock him, insult him, spit on him, flog him and kill him" (Luke 18:33a). That all these things happened, just as he said they would, is known to everyone.

Christianity so identifies its adherents with its founder that there is no cause for surprise in learning that Jesus' disciples are frequently forced to suffer for his sake. The Lord never hid the prospect of suffering from his followers. To the contrary, he explicitly warned of it and cautioned men not to follow him unless they were willing to face cruel and determined opposition. "Blessed are you when people insult you, persecute you and falsely say all kinds of evil against you because of me" (Matt. 5:11). In another setting, he reminded the disciples that "A servant is not greater than his lord" and that persecution for the

65

latter would almost surely guarantee it for the former (John 15:20-21).

Both biblical and non-biblical history testify of the sufferings which early Christians endured. From local persecutions such as the one at Jerusalem under Saul of Tarsus (Acts 8:1ff) to the empire-wide brutalities sponsored by Rome at the end of the century, these saints paid dearly for their faith in and loyalty to Jesus Christ.

First Peter was written to warn and fortify the disciples in the face of a particularly intense persecution which lay ahead shortly. In all likelihood (as indicated in Chapter One), this was the savage tormenting of Christians in and around the capital city under the infamous Nero. Whether the "painful trial" was faced under Nero or (as others think) connected with the fall of Jerusalem a few years later, the principles enunciated can be understood and appreciated by the modern reader.

Peter's Warnings

The apostle looked ahead by the Spirit of God to the things awaiting him and his contemporaries and wrote:

> Dear friends, do not be surprised at the painful trial you are suffering, as though something strange were happening to you. But rejoice that you participate in the sufferings of Christ, so that you may be overjoyed when his glory is revealed. If you are insulted because of the name of Christ, you are blessed, for the Spirit of glory and of God rests on you (1 Pet. 4:12-14; cf. 1:6).

There is nothing surprising (strange, ASV) about suffering in the life of a Christian. In fact, as was observed in the introduction to this lesson, the unusual thing would be its absence.

Why does God allow Christians to be tormented for their faith? Let us answer with another question: Why *shouldn't* he allow it? If Jesus suffered in giving salvation, it is only reasonable to expect to suffer in receiving and living it. If being a Christian eliminated suffering, everyone would become a follower of Jesus – most from an unworthy motive. The suffering one experiences in being a Christian gives him an opportunity to demonstrate his pure motives in embracing Christ.

Remember that whereas all men face trials and challenges simply by virtue of their humanity, the things spoken of in these verses are the additional perils which spring from the fact of devotion to the Lord. Being a Christian does not eliminate suffering, and often it precipitates it. "In fact, everyone who wants to live a godly life in Christ Jesus will be persecuted" (2 Tim. 3:12). Ungodly men oppose the Christian because of his reverence and righteousness. Just as Jesus' presence in the world caused them to strike out against him, the presence of men and women who wear his name and live his truth produces the same reaction against them.

No, it is not surprising that Christians are opposed and persecuted, for "We must go through many hardships to enter the kingdom of God" (Acts 14:22b). The assurance is, however, that having shared in Christ's agony his faithful disciples will also share in his glory when he comes again.

But what of the present needs of a suffering saint? Granted that the future prospect of glory at the second coming is a comfort to him, what aid does he receive in the time of his distress to strengthen and see him through safely? Peter answers that "the Spirit of glory and of God rests on" the suffering people of God.

The "Spirit of glory" and the "Spirit ... of God" are alternate ways of referring to the Holy Spirit. The Spirit is given to the child of God at his conversion (Acts 2:38; 5:32). He abides with those who are persecuted for the sake of encouraging them with his presence. In the eighth chapter of Romans, Paul develops this theme at length. He, like Peter, links the fact that we are to one day be "glorified with" our Savior to the present reality that "we suffer with him" (v. 17). But Christians are not alone in their experience of trials. The Holy Spirit "helps us in our weakness" and "himself intercedes for us" (v. 26). Therefore we can take heart and be confident. "No, in all these things we are more than conquerors through him who loved us" (v. 37).

> If you suffer, it should not be as a murderer or thief or any other kind of criminal, or even as a meddler. However, if you suffer as a Christian, do not be ashamed, but praise God that you bear that name (1 Pet. 4:15-16).

The emphasis of this section is clear. Scripture gives no blanket endorsement of suffering. Some suffering results from an individual's personal sin, and for this there is no divine blessing. Heavenly favor and aid are promised only to those who suffer for the sake of righteousness.

The name "Christian" is a blessed and holy one. It signifies one who belongs to Christ, a citizen of his kingdom. Let no man or woman ever be ashamed to wear it; let none who wear it dishonor that holy name by a sinful life.

In the impending "painful trial," some disciples would be tempted to refuse identification as Christians. A soldier would burst into a house. "The report has come to us that the people of this house are Christians," he would say. "Is the charge true? Is anyone here a Christian?" For people living in or near Rome during Nero's unholy crusade, an affirmative answer could mean death on the spot. What a position of jeopardy! Acknowledge Christ and die; disown him and live. It was at this moment that Jesus' words became so practical as he was remembered to have said, "Do not be afraid of those who kill the body but cannot kill the soul. Rather, be afraid of the One who can destroy both soul and body in hell" (Matt. 10:28). It was at this moment that Peter's plea would ring in the saints' ears: "Don't be ashamed to suffer as a Christian!" All of us would do well to try to visualize our reaction under such a difficult circumstance.

> For it is time for judgment to begin with the family of God; and if it begins with us, what will the outcome be for those who do not obey the gospel of God? And, "If it is hard for the righteous to be saved, what will

become of the ungodly and the sinner?" So then, those who suffer according to God's will should commit themselves to their faithful Creator and continue to do good (1 Pet. 4:17-19).

Trusting God and relying on divine strength in the face of their terrible ordeal, the faithful would be delivered – though "scarcely saved" (ASV) or "saved with great difficulty" (RSV). On the other hand, the person who denied the holy name of Christ would have no hope at all. Thus, in the face of an impending judgment and sifting by persecution, the apostle's admonition is forceful. Bear your suffering bravely. Continue doing what you know to be right. Trust your soul to your faithful Creator.

Nero's Persecution of Saints

To get some idea of what Peter and his fellow saints had to suffer under Nero, we may refer to the writings of a Roman historian of the period. Tacitus describes it in brutally frank language. Since he was unsympathetic to the Christians, his record cannot be dismissed as Christian propaganda which overdraws the picture. A short excerpt from his *Annals* is given in Chapter Six.

Nero ruled the Roman Empire from A.D. 54 to 68. Whereas the first few years of his reign were stable and prosperous, he eventually became a hated man for his excesses and irresponsibility in office. When a great fire broke out at Rome in July of 64, a rumor began to circulate to the effect that Nero had set it. We preserve the rumor today when we speak of "fiddling while Rome burns." The evidence of history is against Nero's being responsible for the fire, and he certainly did not "fiddle" during it. He helped organize fire-fighters; and there were no fiddles in existence.

In order to divert suspicion from himself, he blamed the fire on Christians. Didn't they say that the world was going to end in fire? Christians lost their civil rights. They were beaten, tortured, and murdered. This went on until the non-Christian populace of the city became disgusted with its excesses. Nero was finally condemned to death himself by the Senate but committed suicide before he could be arrested.

Tertullian, writing about the year 200, said that Peter was a victim of this persecution. Origen, as quoted by Eusebius, reflects the same tradition. It is very likely that Paul died in the last stages of the same purge. The need for such an appeal as is found in the text for this study is therefore evident.

Lessons for Today

At the time this book of studies on 1 and 2 Peter is being written, Neronean persecutions are long past. The Western world has religious liberty on an unprecedented scale, and people are not in danger of losing their freedom and lives for wearing the name Christian. So what lessons are to be gained for our situation from this text?

First, we should be grateful for the relative calm of our day and for our religious freedom in particular. Paul exhorted Christians to pray for "kings and all those in authority, that we may live peaceful and quiet lives in all godliness and holiness" (1 Tim. 2:2). We have been given this blessing and have been spared a great trial of our faith and obstacle to our service.

Second, we must use the greater opportunities for work in the kingdom which our peace and freedom provide. When we stop to think how much the early church did in times of intense persecution, it is astounding. Those Christians "turned the world upside down" while everything (on the human side) seemed to be against them. Since responsibility is proportionate to opportunity (cf. Luke 12:48b), surely God is expecting more of us than is being given by the church generally. The evangelistic fervor of those early disciples makes some of us appear totally delinquent.

Third, saints of the present day should fortify our faith against an unknown future. There are forces in the world which would deprive us of our religious liberties if they were to attain power. What would be our reaction to such a thing? How could the church cope with it? Would you be strong enough to follow Jesus through a "painful trial"? If these questions seem remote, one might reflect on the sudden and unanticipated nature of Nero's atrocities. A fire swept the city of Rome and was attributed to Christians. Without warning Roman soldiers began rounding up members of the church. It could happen again.

Fourth, let us be sympathetic with and prayerful for our brothers and sisters in the Lord who are suffering for the name Christian. Living in the freedom of the Western world, we sometimes forget about churches existing in other parts of the world under totalitarian governments which forbid them to assemble, distribute literature, evangelize, etc. Within the past few years, missionaries have been driven out of certain countries, and the fate of Christians still there is unknown to the outside world. We must not fail to pray for these people. "Remember those in prison as if you were their fellow prisoners, and those who are mistreated as if you yourselves were suffering" (Heb. 13:3). While we are blessed with personal liberties in the western world, we must not forget that many are trying to follow Christ in totalitarian countries where they pay a great price in personal suffering.

Fifth, we can be certain that divine aid will sustain the believer in any time of trial. This lesson has dealt with a type of persecution which most of us will never have to face. But among the people who read these pages will be individuals whose families have turned on them because they are Christians, people who have lost their jobs or forfeited promotions because of their convictions, young people whose classmates ridicule their attempt to dress, talk, and behave as Christians, etc. The Spirit of God is within you to strengthen you, make intercession for you, and give you the victory in Jesus. Rejoice, and be bold!

A Summary on Suffering

Because of the experiences Jesus had, we know that our sufferings elicit his compassion. "For we have not a high priest who is unable to sympathize with our weaknesses, but one who in every respect has been tempted as we are, yet without sin" (Heb. 4:15). The God we believe in is "the Father of mercies and God of all comfort" (2 Cor. 1:3). So when bad things happen and we are tempted to lash out at God, accuse him, or think he has forgotten us, let us instead adopt a positive attitude. "Consider it pure joy, my brothers, whenever you face trials of many kinds, because you know that the testing of your faith develops perseverance (steadfastness, RSV)" (Jas. 1:4).

There are no victories without battles. Character develops only as it is tested by the experiences of living. These testing experiences show us our need for God and can drive us closer to him rather than away from him.

God's grace in a believer's life is not intended to save us from trouble. It is intended to save us from defeat. The storms of disappointment, frustration, and sorrow still come to Christians. But we keep on going, and somehow out of those troubles we find ourselves enriched. After the storms, the beauty of life becomes even more beautiful.

In your time of suffering, no one wants to help you more than God. So follow the two steps to victory over trials which Peter marked for his readers: (1) commit yourself to your faithful Creator, and (2) continue to do good (1 Pet. 4:19).

Conclusion

The Christian religion is not an exercise in naive optimism. At the very beginning, its adherents are told of the potential price to be paid for walking in Jesus' steps. Like our Savior, we may have to suffer for our commitment to doing the divine will. There is nothing strange about this, and anyone unwilling to pay the price is not worthy of the name Christian.

In his hour of crisis, the child of God knows he is not alone. He will be comforted and strengthened for the challenge. Even if he should have to die for his faith, he knows of the crown of life which awaits him. He can make whatever sacrifice is necessary to wear the name *Christian*, for he has been given *something to hold on to*.

Chapter Nine

Right Relationships
Are Important

1 Peter 5:1-14

The foremost duty of every person is to establish and maintain a right relationship with God. Jesus told a certain expert in the Law of Moses, "Love the Lord your God with all your heart and with all your soul and with all your mind. This is the first and greatest commandment" (Matt. 22:37-38). Second only to our right relationship with deity, we must also establish and maintain right relationships with our fellowmen. Jesus continued the statement just quoted by saying, "And the second is like it: Love your neighbor as yourself. All the Law and the Prophets hang on these two commandments" (Matt. 22:39-40).

Get right with God; get right with your fellowmen. These two duties are the essence of all the obligations which were imposed on the Jews by means of the Law of Moses.

But these two duties have been at the heart of true religion in every period of history. It is still the case under the gospel of Christ.

Sometimes we place so great an emphasis on getting right with God that we overlook the second commandment. In fact, some people seem to have opted for a type of religion which seeks to appease God while deliberately ignoring the duty of getting right with people around us. For example, it is possible for someone to attend church services faithfully while engaging in dishonest business practices. Another person might use her mouth on Sunday morning to teach the Bible to children and on Monday morning to gossip about her best friend. Still a third could drop a large check into the contribution plate every Lord's Day and be carrying on an affair with his secretary. It is a perverted sort of religious life which allows this sort of duplicity.

One simply cannot be right with God while ignoring right relationships with the people in his world. Paul taught that children are not right with God unless they are being obedient to their parents (cf. Eph. 6:1-3). He said that fathers cannot be right with God unless they are rearing their children according to the principles of righteous living taught in Scripture (cf. Eph. 6:4). He warned both slaves and their masters that the way they treated each other would affect their relationships with God directly (cf. Eph. 6:5-9). And John wrote:

> If anyone says, "I love God," yet hates his brother, he is a liar. For anyone who does not love his brother, whom he has seen, cannot love God, whom he has not seen. And he has given us this command: Whoever loves God must also love his brother (1 John 4:20-21).

Yes, right relationships are important. And this crucial truth which Paul and John emphasized is also stressed by Peter in the epistles he wrote. He, too, attached great importance to the way Christians are supposed to live in community with each other.

Elders and the Local Church

First, there is the matter of elders and their relationship to the local churches they oversee.

> To the elders among you, I appeal as a fellow elder, a witness of Christ's sufferings and one who also will share in the glory to be revealed: Be shepherds of

God's flock that is under your care, serving as over-seers – not because you must, but because you are willing, as God wants you to be; not greedy for money, but eager to serve; not lording it over those entrusted to you, but being examples to the flock. And when the Chief Shepherd appears, you will receive the crown of glory that will never fade away (1 Pet. 5:1-4).

Under Christ and the apostles, elders have the responsibility of leading the local church in fulfilling its mission in the world. In the first century, the apostles ordained elders in every church (Acts 14:23; cf. Tit. 1:5). These men had the responsibility of overseeing the spiritual life of the various congregations and guarding them from false teachers (Acts 20:28-29). They administered the finances of the churches (Acts 11:30). They took personal interest in the welfare of every soul under their charge (Jas. 5:14).

Although Peter was an apostle, he based this appeal to elders on the fact that he was an elder, too. He wanted his fellow elders to take their responsibilities seriously. He wanted them to be in right relationship with the souls for whom they were responsible. Such a relationship depends on the following things:

(1) They must oversee the church. Elders do a disserv-ice to the members of a congregation when they view their office as honorary rather than functional. They must ac-tually take charge of the church's affairs so as to provide such leadership as will harness its energies into produc-tive channels.

(2) They must use their divinely given authority in the right way and with proper motives. Elders must assume the oversight "not because you must, but because you are willing, as God wants you to be." This means that such men must fulfill their duties with a sense of grateful ea-gerness and not under coercion; their work is not to be performed as a grim and burdensome duty but as a happy privilege. After all, the first qualification of an elder is that he must desire and seek the office (1 Tim. 3:1). This does not allow a man to grab for or campaign to become an

75

elder, but it does mean that if the members of a congregation ask him to serve in this capacity he should do so with humble yet eager willingness.

Although some elders of the early church were supported financially for the performance of their work (cf. 1 Tim. 5:17-18) and such men may be so supported today, Peter warned against serving for the sake of the money involved (cf. 1 Tim. 3:3; Tit. 1:7). Neither are elders to be puffed up with pride over their authority so as to be found "lording it over those entrusted to you."

(3) Instead, they must lead not so much by virtue of their position as by example. The leadership style of Jesus Christ was startling to the people who observed it. It continues to confuse most of us. And hardly anyone is willing to adopt it. He did not lead people by coercion and threats. He did not appeal to institutionalized authority or give people around him the impression of being subordinates and flunkies. He never violated another person's freedom and right to make choices.

The Lord Jesus explained his attitude toward spiritual leadership by saying: "Whoever wants to become great among you must be your servant, and whoever wants to be first must be your slave" (cf. Matt. 20:25-28). Elders, deacons, teachers, preachers, and other leaders in fields of Christian endeavor must take our cues for leadership from Jesus rather than the world.

You know a powerful person in the world by the number of heads he/she turns, people he/she intimidates, and policies he/she railroads over others. You know a leader in the kingdom of God by the unassuming service he/she renders, people he/she ministers to, and discomfort he/she feels when someone takes notice of what has been done and offers praise for it.

A few years ago there was a series of exchanges in brotherhood papers about the authority of elders. It was so much wasted ink, paper, and energy. Of course elders have authority. That's not the issue. The real question is: What is the nature of an elder's authority? Answer: He has authority to serve, minister, heal, teach, and otherwise spend himself for others; he does not have authority to boss, lord, coerce, and otherwise throw around his title and position as a means of intimidation. Yes, Jesus' leadership style is so very different from the one carnal man understands and admires that it is difficult to adopt. But it is the only one appropriate to the kingdom of God.

It is not only important for elders to relate to the congregation properly. The congregation must have a proper relationship to them. "Obey your leaders and submit to their authority. They keep watch over you as men who must give an account" (Heb. 13:17a).

So many problems would never arise if the eldership-membership association worked properly. Willing and active leadership would challenge the church to fruitful work; responsive members would apply their energies to the implementation of sound ideas. Unity and progress in the gospel would result. Yes, right relationships are important.

Interdependence of Christians

Second, Peter spoke to the more general matter of right relationships among the total membership of local churches. The healthy church is like a healthy body. Every member functions in concert with every other member. Jealousy and competition are unthinkable. An interdependent community of Christians has been formed to serve under Jesus Christ, the head of the body. Here are four virtues extolled by the Holy Spirit through Peter which help the body maintain health.

Respect for older members. "Young men, in the same way be submissive to those who are older" (1 Pet. 5:5a). It seems likely that Peter's exhortation here has to do with the relationship of younger Christians to older ones in general rather than to the men in office as elders in particular.

The present generation tends to idolize youth and despise old age. How wrong we are. There is a wisdom which can come only from having lived, and those who are younger would be wise to seek the counsel of the old on more matters. In the membership of the church, older saints who are veterans in the service of the Lord deserve special honor. They have carried the burden in the past, and now that they are unable to be as active as they once were it is crass and mean to make them feel unwanted.

Humility. "All of you, clothe yourselves with humility toward one another, because, 'God opposes the proud, but gives grace to the humble.' Humble yourselves, therefore, under God's mighty hand, that he may lift you up in due time" (1 Pet. 5:5b-6).

Pride makes right relationships among human beings impossible. The proud person insists on his own way, treats others as if they existed only for his selfish purposes, and refuses to extend himself on behalf of someone else. His ego is too large for his spiritual well-being.

Peter had had his ego deflated in a most vivid scene on the night of Jesus' betrayal. Having come into the upper room with Jesus and the other apostles to eat their last Passover meal together, no one volunteered to perform the servant's role of washing the feet of the guests. It was beneath their dignity. So Jesus himself took a towel, girded himself, and washed their feet. How embarrassed the entire group must have been. This lesson on humility surely stayed in the mind of Peter, and the very language he used in passing it on to his readers here is reminiscent of that scene. Just as the Lord clothed himself humbly with a towel to wash the feet of his followers, so must we be willing to gird ourselves with humility to serve one another. Heaven gives preference to the humble man over the proud (cf. Prov. 3:34), for he alone can render reverent obedience to God and show due respect and consideration for his fellows.

Calm Assurance. "Cast all your anxiety on him because he cares for you" (1 Pet. 5:7). Anxiety is not only an evidence of little faith in God (cf. Matt. 6:31-32) but is also a source of strife and contention between the person who is worried and his associates. What happens when you are worried about something? You get irritable, touchy, and short-tempered. Such a disposition makes right relationships impossible.

How much better is it, then, to cast your worries on the Lord. Take him at his word that no problem will ever come to you that is too great for you to bear (cf. 1 Cor. 10:13). So long as you build your life on the solid foundation of hearing and doing the will of God, the storms of life cannot destroy you (cf. Matt. 7:24-27). Commit your cares to him in trusting prayer, and "do not worry about tomorrow" (Matt. 6:34a).

Vigilance. "Be self-controlled and alert. Your enemy the devil prowls around like a roaring lion looking for someone to devour. Resist him, standing firm in the faith, because you know that your brothers throughout the world are undergoing the same kind of sufferings" (1 Pet. 5:8-9).

Earlier in the text for this lesson, Peter has presented Jesus as the Chief Shepherd and the church as his flock. Now he has gone back to that analogy to remind us of the activity of the arch-enemy of our souls. If we are the Lord's little lambs, Satan is a vicious lion ready to pounce on the one of us who strays away from the fold. We have been warned of his activity, and it is our duty to be on guard constantly.

One of the devil's most effective tactics in snaring souls is to disrupt the community of the saints. Let some sister get her feelings hurt and stop coming to the assemblies, and Satan will get her. Let some worried and ill-tempered man take some remark of the teacher as a personal affront, and he is in danger of being trapped by the devil. Yes, right relationships are important.

Some Personal Relationships of Peter

Finally in his first epistle, Peter speaks of some important relationships in his personal life and ministry. He writes of his concern for the people who are the immediate recipients of the epistle; he names certain co-workers who were helping him in his ministry.

On behalf of his readers, he offered this prayer:

> And the God of all grace, who called you to his eternal glory in Christ, after you have suffered a little while, will himself restore you and make you strong, firm and steadfast. To him be the power for ever and ever. Amen (1 Pet. 5:10-11).

From the start of our study of these epistles, the theme of suffering for Christ has been present. Various motives have been appealed to in an effort to fortify the resolve of the first-century readers who would have to endure terrible perseuctions and even death for the sake of their faith. Here, however, Peter asks his readers to look beyond the immediate prospect of suffering to the results which would come from faithful endurance. He prays that God will "restore you and make you strong, firm and steadfast."

Notice the very beautiful progression envisioned in the prayerful desire.

(1) By virtue of one's faithful endurance of suffering, heaven will *restore* a child of God. The Greek word so translated refers to the healing of something broken or the supplying of something which is lacking. The point is that God can use suffering to enrich a person and build graces into his life which have been lacking. As a result, like a body healed after an accident, the person is restored to wholeness. For example, the calloused indifference of a young and healthy person to the need of the elderly and sick may be altered only by some tragedy he experiences which softens his heart and broadens his sympathies. A grace has been added to the person's character through suffering which has restored him to good spiritual health.

(2) By virtue of the experience of suffering, God will make one *strong*. Suffering can take a vacillating person like Peter (during Jesus' public ministry) and turn him into a staunch and powerful defender of the faith (following the resurrection). In fact, in prophesying of Peter's experience relative to his death and resurrection, Jesus used the very same word found here. "When you have turned

back," said the Lord, "strengthen your brothers" (Luke 22:32).

(3) By virtue of suffering, the Lord will make the person who endures *firm*. The individual who does not exercise his body will grow flabby and weak; exertion and discipline can restore muscle tone and firmness. The same is true of one's spirit. Faith that has come through loss, disappointment, and pain can be leaner and firmer for having passed through the ordeal.

(4) Endurance of suffering also allows the Lord to make a person *steadfast*. Suffering forces us to find the deep and essential elements of Christian faith. At such a point, one's life is founded on the bedrock of divine truth and grace, and such a life is settled, secure, and steadfast with God.

Yes, suffering can destroy; it can breed resentment, doubt, and bitterness. But there is no reason why it must produce such a result. If we understand that suffering is an essential part of the godly life (cf. 2 Tim. 3:12) and react to it in child-like trust, spiritual benefits will result which otherwise would have been forfeited. Peter's hope was that his readers would allow God to use their experience of suffering to bring about those benefits in their lives.

At this point, he closed the first epistle with these words:

> With the help of Silas, whom I regard as a faithful brother, I have written to you briefly, encouraging you and testifying that this is the true grace of God. Stand fast in it.
>
> She who is in Babylon, chosen together with you, sends you her greetings, and so does my son Mark. Greet one another with a kiss of love.
>
> Peace to all of you who are in Christ (1 Pet. 5:12-14).

Here he identifies Silas as his assistant in writing the letter. This could mean either that he was the penman for Peter or that he carried the letter to the apostle's intended readers or both. This is almost surely the same man who was Paul's frequent assistant (cf. Acts 15:37ff; 1 Thess. 1:1; *et al.*).

Next he sends greetings from the church at Rome.

Finally, he joins the name of Mark with the closing of the epistle. Mark, the author of the second Gospel, is closely identified with Peter in the early traditions of the church and must have had the kind of relationship with Peter that Timothy had with Paul (cf. 2 Tim. 1:2).

Conclusion

The special fellowship which is the church constitutes a unique blessing of God to his children. The "kiss of love" and the "peace" of Christ are particular aspects of this fellowship which are mentioned at the close of the letter.

May we be wise enough in our generation to foster and cherish this fellowship. After all, right relationships are not only important but are also *something to hold on to.*

Chapter Ten

Your Calling and Election

2 Peter 1:3-11

The Bible teaches that election and predestination are involved in the process of salvation. For example, Paul writes of those whom God "foreknew" and "predestined to be conformed to the likeness of his Son" (Rom. 8:29-30). Again, writing the prison epistle we call Ephesians, he spoke of those whom God "chose ... before the creation of the world" and who had been lovingly "predestined" to be adopted into the family of God (Eph. 1:4-5).

Some people interpret these and related passages to mean that God elects and predestines certain *specific individuals* to be saved or lost. Following Augustine and John Calvin, they insist that the number of people to be saved has been fixed in heaven from eternity and that nothing we may do on earth can alter the fates we have been assigned.

If such a doctrine were true, think of some of the absurd consequences which would follow. For one thing, how could the Bible declare that "God does not show favoritism" with his human creatures (Acts 10:34b) if he has arbitrarily selected some people to be saved while passing over (or consciously rejecting) all others? For another, why would Jesus teach that men can choose their own destinies if it is not so? He challenges men and women to make a choice between two gates, one leading to eternal life and one leading to destruction (Matt. 7:13-14). Again, the words of Peter would be meaningless if such a doctrine were true: "Save yourselves from this corrupt generation" (Acts 2:40b). If salvation is altogether due to divine election of an individual, there is no sense at all in which anyone can save himself.

The truth of the matter is that God has foreordained that a certain *group* of people will be saved (i.e., those who are "in Christ," cf. Eph. 1:4) and leaves it up to each individual to choose whether or not to be included in this number.

Listening to a man on radio as I drove down the highway several years ago, he explained the doctrine of "election" in this rather crude but basically correct way. He said,

> As we understand the term "election," it has to do with voting on a candidate. Well, in this case, *you* are the candidate and the "office" in view is salvation. God has voted *for* you; Satan has voted *against* you. Now it is up to you to cast the deciding ballot. You can either vote with God by learning and obeying his Word, or you can vote with the devil by remaining in your sinful ways. It is your vote that swings the election.

While this is a rather unsophisticated explanation of a complex and profound subject, it does make a crucial point: being saved or lost is ultimately the choice of each person for himself.

From a careful study of the Scripture, the following points emerge which are relevant to this topic. (1) God wants all men to be saved (cf. 2: Pet. 3:9; 1 Tim. 2:4). (2) The gospel is heaven's means of calling all men unto salvation and eternal life (cf. 2 Thess. 2:14). (3) The person who hears and obeys the gospel is saved in connection with that submissive response of faith to the grace of God (cf. Matt. 7:21; Heb. 5:8-9), whereas the one who does not obey the gospel remains in his sin and condemnation (cf. 2 Thess. 1:8).

In 2 Peter 1:3-11, the apostle tells his readers how to "make your calling and election sure." There can be no doubt that he regards the divine election to salvation as a conditional one; the Christian's salvation is "sure" only *if* he responds in true faith to God's will. When he does so, however, the assurance is that "you will never fall."

The Promises of God

As with all good things (cf. Jas. 1:17), salvation begins with the generosity of God. It is by grace and has been made possible only because of the substitutionary death of Jesus on the cross.

> His divine power has given us everything we need for life and godliness through our knowledge of him who called us by his own glory and goodness. Through these he has given us his very great and precious promises, so that through them you may participate in the divine nature and escape the corruption in the world caused by evil desires (2 Pet. 1:3-4).

The people to whom Peter wrote this epistle were like most of the people who will ever read this book. They were baptized believers in Christ who needed reassurance concerning their ability to live a godly life and to get safely home to heaven. On what basis can such confidence be built?

It cannot be founded on ourselves, viz., our strength, our goodness, our effort. How often have we Christians been weak when we thought we were strong! No, assurance that we are among the "elect" must rest on a firmer base than personal self-confidence.

Indeed, Peter does not appeal to belief in self in his effort to inspire his readers to confidence. He appeals to our knowledge of God's flawless record as a keeper of promises. How do we know we have the victory over the world's corruption? How can we be partakers of the divine nature? We have God's sure word on the matter.

In the days of Noah, God promised that he would send a destructive flood to destroy impenitent sinners. Time passed, and men began to scoff. They were sure that God either did not mean what he said or had forgotten his promise. Did the promise fail? You know the answer.

To his servant Abraham, God promised a son. But both he and his wife were old and well beyond the age of having children. Could it be? Just as with Noah's case, the fulfillment did not come on the same day as the promise. Would God keep his word? The life of Isaac is proof that God always makes his promises good.

On and on this listing of fulfilled promises could go. God *always* does what he says he will do.

We, too, have been promised something by this faithful God. He has given us his *very great* and *precious* promises. On the basis of these promises, we are assured of being participants in the divine nature and escaping the world's defilements and evil desires.

What are some of the specific promises of God which apply to us? He promised to forgive our sins at baptism (Acts 2:38). He said he would count us as his own sons from that time forward (Gal. 3:26-27). He pledged the indwelling presence of the Holy Spirit to strengthen us against Satan (Acts 5:32; Eph. 3:16). He promised that no overbearing temptation would be allowed to come against us (1 Cor. 10:13). He has assured us that he would hear our prayers, forgive our sins, and do so many other things. This is the basis of our confidence. We are confident because our God keeps his promises.

However, God's promises to his children are in the form of a *covenant* he has made with us. And, as with most covenants, there are *mutual obligations* in this relationship. He will keep his part of the covenant, and we must be faithful to ours.

The Duty of Man

The essence of the Christian's covenantal responsibility to God is continued growth in spiritual things. Salvation is grounded in the finished work of Christ, and we do not contribute one thing to his redemptive sufferings. We simply grow in love for him and increase our likeness to him in this evil world's environment. The faith which brought us to salvation must be supplemented with other graces.

> For this very reason, make every effort to add to your faith goodness; and to goodness, knowledge; and to knowledge, self-control; and to self-control, perseverance; and to perseverance, godliness; and to godliness, brotherly kindness; and to brotherly kindness, love (2 Pet. 1:5-7).

Look briefly at each of these so-called Christian Graces.

Faith is the foundation for all these qualities. In its essential nature, "faith is being sure of what we hope for and certain of what we do not see" (Heb. 11:1). It is on the basis of such an attitude of certainty toward God's word that one is willing to go still further into spiritual things. He knows the promised result will come.

Goodness (virtue, ASV) is translated from the Greek word *arete*, a word used infrequently in the New Testament. It occurs rather often, however, in the writings of Plato, where it is usually rendered by the word "excellence." The word refers to moral excellence and to the kind of courage which is necessary for doing what one knows to be right.

Knowledge is intended to be the guide for moral excellence and courage. Here the word signifies practical acquaintance with the will of Christ. "Therefore do not be foolish, but understand what the Lord's will is" (Eph. 5:17). It is on the basis of this knowledge that the child of God makes his decisions and orders his life.

Self-control (temperance, KJV) refers to the mastery of our appetites and desires. It is the grace which checks such evils as covetousness, sensuality, etc.

Perseverance (patience, ASV) is the ability not only to endure difficulties but to face up to them in a positive way so as to turn them into opportunities. "Consider it pure joy, my brothers, whenever you face trials of many kinds, because you know that the testing of your faith develops perseverance" (Jas. 1:2-3).

Godliness denotes an attitude of heart which bows in willing submission to deity. It embraces the same concept of reverence which is included in the Old Testament expression "the fear of the Lord."

Brotherly kindness is that attitude of special concern that Christians are to foster for one another. Because we are children of God, we are brothers and sisters to one another. Therefore: "Be devoted to one another in brotherly love. Honor one another before yourselves" (Rom. 12:10).

Finally, *love* is the crowning grace. Christian love (Gk., *agape*) is the willingness to put another's happiness or well-being above one's own; it is the willingness to sacrifice oneself for the sake of the other person. Jesus' "new commandment" to his disciples was to require that we love one another in the way he has already loved all of us; this, he said, would be our badge of discipleship by which all who observed us would know we belonged to him (John 13:34-35).

What a challenge it is to supply more of these graces daily. What blessedness comes to the person who does grow in these qualities. On the other hand, the Christian who takes these things for granted and doesn't consciously add these graces to his life is headed for spiritual disaster.

> For if you possess these qualities in increasing measure, they will keep you from being ineffective and unproductive in your knowledge of our Lord Jesus Christ. But if anyone does not have them he is near-sighted and blind, and has forgotten that he has been cleansed from his past sins (2 Pet. 1:8-9).

The Confidence of Salvation

Now that Peter has spoken of God's gracious promises to his people and has described the growth process which occurs in the life of the faithful, he is in position to give

88

his readers the assurance they need about their spiritual status.

> Therefore, my brothers, be all the more eager to make your calling and election sure. For if you do these things, you will never fall, and you will receive a rich welcome into the eternal kingdom of our Lord and Savior Jesus Christ (2 Pet. 1:10-11).

Can a Christian be confident about eternal life? Can he know he is saved? Of course he can! After all, salvation is not a mystical gift given and taken at the whim of an irrational god. It is not something capriciously given to a few and denied all the rest of mankind. It is offered to all, and each of us is able to know whether or not he has accepted this free gift.

Have you turned away from all your sins and been buried with Christ in the watery grave of baptism? Are you walking in the light of divine truth, adding these Christian graces to your character daily? If so, you are saved; you are taking care to "make your calling and election *sure.*"

Some people teach the false doctrine of unconditional security. This doctrine holds that if a person is truly saved, he can never so sin as to be lost. He is saved, and saved unconditionally. Such a view of things offers false security. Inspired counsel on this matter offers real security in relation to a reasonable test of faith. "*If* you do these things, *you will never fall.*" This does not eliminate grace or make salvation a matter of human merit; it does provide a realistic means of knowing where one stands in relation to God.

Salvation is yours unless you choose to walk away from it. So long as you walk in it, evidences of growth and maturity will be forthcoming.

Conclusion

The divine role in salvation is the great and difficult one. Heaven had to extend itself to the ultimate limits of love in order to provide the very Son of God as a sacrificial offering for sinful humanity. The love and grace of God provided a means for our justification. In the person of Jesus Christ, deity came among men and provided full atonement. The blood of the Son of God is powerful enough to wash away sin. Heaven has published this good news to mankind through the gospel and is calling everyone to be saved.

This does not mean, unfortunately, that all men will be saved. There is a human response of faith that must be made to the gospel of God's grace. Some people refuse to believe on him. Others have a faith that is so impotent as to be dead; it will not motivate them to repentance, baptism, and holy living. Others, though, have a living faith which reaches out in loving gratitude to take hold of, embrace, and live the gospel.

Here, then, is a practical and measurable test of faith in the life of a child of God. Here is a practical means of assurance on the basis of identifiable Christian Graces which are fostered in the life of God's faithful children and which give the Christian *something to hold on to.*

Chapter Eleven

The Certainty of God's Word

2 Peter 1:12-21

The apostle Peter put great stress on the reliability of the Word of God. Both in his own writings and in his recorded sermons, he frequently called attention to the divine faithfulness with regard to statements and promises.

In the sermon he preached on the first Pentecost following the resurrection of Christ, Peter appealed to the testimony of Old Testament prophecies to establish the messiahship of Jesus. To explain the phenomena connected with the coming of the Holy Spirit on that day, he quoted the prophecy of Joel 2:28ff (Acts 2:15-21); in support of his claim that Jesus had risen from the dead, he quoted Psalm 16:8ff (Acts 2:24-28); with reference to Christ's exaltation at the right hand of the Father, he said this, too, was in fulfillment of a prophecy to raise up someone from among David's descendants to reign upon his throne (Acts 2:30-31; cf. 2 Sam. 7:12-16). This sermon set the pattern for apologetic preaching to the Jews throughout Acts. Old Testament prophecies were shown to be fulfilled in Jesus, and this was offered as proof of the truthfulness of his claims to be the Messiah and Son of God.

Peter stressed this same theme in his first epistle.

Concerning this salvation, the prophets, who spoke of the grace that was to come to you, searched intently and with the greatest care, trying to find out the time and circumstances to which the Spirit of Christ in them was pointing when he predicted the sufferings of Christ and the glories that would follow.

It was revealed to them that they were not serving themselves but you, when they spoke of the things that have now been told you by those who have preached the gospel to you by the Holy Spirit sent from heaven. Even angels long to look into these things (2 Pet. 1:10-12).

Earlier in the second epistle, he has already called attention to God's "very great and and precious promises" (1:4) as the basis for our assurance of salvation. But in the text to be studied in this lesson, he develops the theme even further.

The Importance of Being Certain

Christianity is an historical religion. Its truth claims center around real events which occurred in space and time on this planet. Jesus was a real man who lived at a certain time and in a certain place; it is claimed that he was virgin born and raised bodily from the dead. These events, since they occurred in history, are subject to the same tests as other alleged events of the past. If they pass those tests, we have a basis for confidence and faith; if they do not, we must either abandon them as false or practice willful self-deception.

The evangelists of the early church proclaimed the gospel in the certainty that it was true. Writing now as an old man and veteran of the faith, Peter was still anxious to recall the gospel facts for the sake of his readers.

So I will always remind you of these things, even though you know them and are firmly established in the truth you now have. I think it is right to refresh your memory as long as I live in the tent of this body, because I know that I will soon put it aside, as our Lord Jesus Christ has made clear to me. And I will make every effort to see that after my departure you will always be able to remember these things (2 Pet. 1:12-15).

Certainty about Christ was the source of Peter's devotion to the gospel and service in the church. Doubt and deadness go together; certainty, on the other hand, breeds vigor and earnestness. The old apostle had not lived for a lie.

In the twentieth century, skepticism seems to be in the very air we breathe and is often presented as a sign of wisdom. Many liberal theologians flatly deny the factuality of the virgin birth and bodily resurrection; they say the Bible is generally untrustworthy as a source of factual data. Some theologial systems even glory in their uncertainty and insist that the essence of faith is in trusting oneself to something in the absence of certainty about it.

What a far cry from the certain ring of New Testament preaching. Faith and knowledge are not mutually exclusive. Peter himself had said to Jesus, "We *believe* and *know* that you are the Holy One of God" (John 6:69). Paul wrote: "I am not ashamed, because I *know* whom I have *believed*, and am *convinced* that he is able to guard what I have entrusted to him for that day" (2 Tim. 1:12b). A precise translation of Hebrews 11:1 underscores the certainty which is the hallmark of biblical faith: "Now faith is being sure of what we hope for and certain of what we do not see" (NIV). The words translated "being sure" and "certain" in this passage are strong terms which denote something settled and proved beyond doubt.

In a long article on faith, the *Theological Dictionary of the New Testament* observes:

> In respect of their objects, there is no difference between *pisteuein* (to believe) and *ginoskein* (to know). ... The fact that either is possible shows that *pisteuein* and *ginoskein* are not simply to be differ-

entiated as initial and final stages, and it certainly rules out any distinction into two kinds of Christians, the pistics and the gnostics, as in Christian Gnosticism. In antithesis to Gnosticism it is apparent that knowledge can never take us beyond faith or leave faith behind (VI: 227).

Perhaps the lethargy and deadness which we lament among some Christians of our day is traceable directly to a lack of certainty about fundamental doctrines of the Bible. What we need is not psychological hoopla but strong apologetic preaching which sets forth the biblical claims and competently presents the evidence which establishes them.

The Basis of Peter's Certainty

Peter attributes his personal certainty about Jesus to three things.

First, he was an *eyewitness* to the divine majesty of the Lord.

> We did not follow cleverly invented stories when we told you about the power and coming of our Lord Jesus Christ, but we were eyewitnesses of his majesty (2 Pet. 1:16).

Contemporary theologians speak of Christianity in terms of "powerful myth." By this they mean that it expresses in a symbolic way certain deep insights into man and his world. One who accepts the perspective of Peter on the nature of true religion reacts to such an explanation with abhorrence. He denied that what he preached were "cleverly invented stories" (fables, ASV). To the contrary, he was speaking of things he had seen with his own eyes. With his fellow apostle, John, he told of things "which we have heard, which we have seen with our eyes, which we have looked at and our hands have touched" (1 John 1:1).

The specific event in Peter's mind at this point was the Transfiguration (Matt. 17:1-13). On that extraordinary occasion, Peter, along with James and John, accompanied the Lord into a high mountain where Jesus "was transfigured before them"; his face "shone like the sun" and his clothing "became as white as the light." The three apostles also saw Moses and Elijah, the great lawgiver and the outstanding prophet of days gone by, as they appeared and talked with the Son of Man about his impending death at Jerusalem (Luke 9:31).

This sight burned itself into the memory of Peter. It, along with many other events to which he was an eyewitness, left no possibility of doubt in his mind as to the identity of the Son of God.

Second, he not only saw the Son transfigured but also *heard the Father's voice* speak from heaven to identify Jesus.

> For he received honor and glory from God the Father when the voice came to him from the Majestic Glory, saying, "This is my Son, whom I love; with him I am well pleased." We ourselves heard this voice that came from heaven when we were with him on the sacred mountain (2 Pet. 1:17-18).

This occurred, of course, at the time of the Transfiguration (Matt. 17:5).

Could it have been a dream? Might Peter have had an hallucination? Surely such possibilities occurred to Peter himself. But he had been able to resolve these questions by "comparing notes" with James and John. As he emphasizes in our text, they all saw and they all heard the same things. One man might have a dream or hallucinate. Three men do not have an identical dream or hallucination simultaneously.

Third, he had the testimony of the *prophetic word* as proof of the truthfulness of Christ's claims about himself. "And we have the word of the prophets made more certain" (2 Pet. 1:19a).

Throughout his ministry, Jesus called attention to the fact that the events of his life were fulfilling Old Testament prophecies about the Messiah. As Jesus and the three apostles were coming down from the mount of Transfiguration, for example, he reminded them of the prophecies about the ministry of John the Baptizer and his own suffering (Mark 9:12-13). At the Last Supper, he reminded all the apostles that his betrayal by a friend had been predicted in Scripture (Matt. 26:24). Then after the resurrection he discussed many of these prophecies with them. "Then he opened their minds so they could understand the Scriptures. He told them, 'This is what is written: The Christ will suffer and rise from the dead on the third day'" (Luke 24:45-46).

As was pointed out earlier in this chapter, Peter and the other evangelists of the church used this same approach in their preaching. Whenever they were among Jewish people who knew the Old Testament, they appealed to the phenomenon of fulfilled prophecy to establish their claims about Jesus. As one of the men who had personally witnessed many of the fulfillments come to pass, Peter had had these prophecies confirmed (i.e., "made more certain") to him and could not fail to proclaim Jesus as Lord and Christ on this basis.

Giving Heed to Scripture

One of the early readers of this epistle might be ready to object at this point: "That is all to your benefit, Peter. You can have certainty concerning Jesus because of your personal contact with him. You touched him, saw him work miracles, heard the Father endorse his claims by speaking from heaven, and were with him after the resurrection. But what of us who have had no such direct contact with him? How may we be certain about him?"

It is questions of this nature that he answers in the final section of chapter one.

... and you will do well to pay attention to it [i.e., the prophetic word], as to a light shining in a dark place, until the day dawns and the morning star rises in your hearts. Above all, you must understand that no prophecy of Scripture came about by the prophet's own interpretation. For prophecy never had its origin in the will of man, but men spoke from God as they were carried along by the Holy Spirit (2 Pet. 1:19b-21).

For most of the apostle's first readers and for all of us who read him today, there is one and only one means to certain knowledge about the Son of God. We can give attention to the divine Word of God which testifies concerning Jesus, test its assertions for logical consistency and historical trustworthiness, and draw such conclusions as are warranted by the evidence. Such study of the prophetic word will have the same effect as a "light shining in a dark place." The darkness of ignorance and doubt will give way to the dawning day.

But can our knowledge of Jesus be as certain as that of the people who had direct contact with him? Those of us who do not have the same first-hand evidence Peter had are not in a situation of necessary disadvantage. He had the direct evidence of sensory experience, i.e., he saw and heard certain things involving Jesus. We have the indirect evidence of testimony from numerous eyewitnesses, historical data from both biblical and non-biblical sources, prophecies and their clear fulfillments, etc. To say that someone in the latter situation can never be as certain as the person in the former situation is to say that no jury has ever rendered a true and certain verdict on the basis of the evidence presented to it.

Someone objects again, "But juries have been known to make mistakes." Yes, and eyewitnesses have also been known to identify the wrong person. So whether one's evidence is direct or indirect, he must take care with it.

First, whether one has direct or indirect evidence, he must reason correctly about the data. That is, he must follow the rules of logic and historical investigation.

Second, one cannot say that sensory experience is always preferable over indirect evidences, for our senses sometimes deceive us. Have you ever seen a pencil in a glass of water?

Third, evaluating testimony from several witnesses, along

with whatever other evidence may be relevant to the inquiry, is often better than being an eyewitness. Frequently it happens that eyewitnesses disagree, and objective third parties have to sift and test their statements in order to arrive at certainty.

Fourth, not everyone who had direct (i.e., eyewitness) evidence about Jesus drew the same conclusion Peter did. Judas and others saw the miracles and heard the teachings of the Lord and still rejected him. This fact alone proves that certainty is not directly related to whether one's evidence is direct or indirect.

Fifth, the Bible itself says that the testimony of Scripture is sometimes (if not generally) superior to evidence which comes through the senses. Abraham told the rich man that if his brothers back on the earth would not accept the testimony of Moses and the prophets (i.e., the Old Testament), neither would they be persuaded by having someone come back from the dead to warn them about meeting God (Luke 16:27-31).

Since Scripture did not originate with men (i.e., it is not "the prophet's own interpretation"), its testimony on any matter is the surest of all evidences. Its contents were written by men who were "carried along by the Holy Spirit." As Paul expressed it, "All Scripture is God-breathed ..." (2 Tim. 3:16). When we hear, examine, and receive the testimony of the Word of God on a matter, we have absolute certainty on that matter; our faith in that testimony provides knowledge of God's will.

Conclusion

In the absence of certainty, there is always room for doubt, hesitation, and holding back. It is the sweeping away of doubt that produces boldness and vigor in service to the Lord.

Consider the case of Thomas. At first he doubted the resurrection and hesitated to join with the other apostles in joy and praise. Jesus appeared to him eight days after the resurrection. He challenged Thomas to reach out and

98

touch his hands and side in order to examine the sites of the wounds he received in the crucifixion. This would provide first-hand evidence that the same Jesus he had seen die was now alive again. Thomas saw, believed, and exclaimed, "My Lord and my God!" (John 20:27-28).

Jesus' response to this confession is interesting in light of the study of our text for this chapter. "Then Jesus told him, 'Because you have seen me, you have believed; blessed are those who have not seen and yet have believed'" (John 20:29). Thomas came to certainty and boldness by *seeing* Jesus alive again; we can come to that same certainty and boldness by *faith*. Indeed, "we live by faith, not by sight" (2 Cor. 5:7).

Faith and knowledge are never contrasted in the Word of God. To the contrary, both sight (i.e., direct acquaintance with certain facts through the senses) and faith (i.e., indirect acquaintance with those facts through testimony) are means to the same goal, viz., *knowledge* of God and his will. Thus Peter bids us to take heed to the word of prophecy (cf. Rom. 10:17) as *something to hold on to.*

Chapter Twelve

Perils from False Teachers

2 Peter 2:1-22

False teachers have plagued the work of God in every age of the history of the world. They will continue to surface and do their damning work until the Lord comes again. For this reason, people who love the Lord must be on their guard constantly.

The divine attitude toward people who would pervert the truth of God has always been the same. Under the Law of Moses, it was decreed that false prophets should be put to death. "But a prophet who presumes to speak in my name anything I have not commanded him to say, or a prophet who speaks in the name of other gods, must be put to death" (Deut. 18:20). During the time of his personal ministry, Jesus had this to say to false teachers of the Law: "Woe to you, teachers of the law and Pharisees, you hypocrites! You travel over land and sea to win a single convert, and when he becomes one, you make him twice as much a son of hell as you are" (Matt. 23:15). And Paul wrote of false teachers: "If anybody is preaching to you a gospel other than what you accepted, let him be eternally condemned!" (Gal. 1:9).

Some situations call for patience and forbearance and tolerance, but the working of a false teacher is not one of those situations. False teachers are to be opposed and stopped.

There is no more scathing rebuke of false teachers anywhere in the Word of God than the one found in the second chapter of 2 Peter.

A Warning About False Teachers

The opening words of the chapter sound a clear note of warning.

> But there were also false prophets among the people, just as there will be false teachers among you. They will secretly introduce destructive heresies, even denying the sovereign Lord who bought them – bringing swift destruction on themselves. Many will follow their shameful ways and will bring the way of truth into disrepute. In their greed these teachers will exploit you with stories they have made up. Their condemnation has long been hanging over them, and their destruction has not been sleeping (2 Pet. 2:1-3).

Peter warned that false prophets would arise among Christians in the same way they had among the Israelites. Indeed, they had already begun to appear when he wrote this epistle. For example, Paul had earlier written of "false brothers" (cf. Gal. 2:4) and "false apostles" (cf. 2 Cor. 11:13). Such men never present themselves for what they really are. They are "savage wolves ... [who] distort the truth in order to draw away disciples after them" (Acts 20:29-30), yet they make their entrance as saints and angels of light. And so they must, for who would follow the man who admitted to being a wrecker of faith and perverter of morals?

They may choose such noble banners as "love" or "scholarship" under which to march, but they prostitute such words for the sake of secretly bringing in their "destructive heresies." Surely the words of Jesus himself are behind the apostle's opening appeal: "Watch out for false prophets. They come to you in sheep's clothing, but inwardly they are ferocious wolves" (Matt. 7:15).

False teachers can always get a following, for some men do not love the truth (cf. 2 Thess. 2:12). Some people dislike the strict moral purity which the gospel requires; they will gladly follow the false teacher's "shameful ways." Others long for novelty; they will quickly latch onto any new theory that is propounded. Still more want the attention, fame, and wealth that can be attained by means of false religion. Indeed, more "sheep" have been "fleeced" by cultists and religious charlatans than by strong-arm robbers. They will jump on the bandwagon for the prospect of sharing in the proceeds. The Manson cult, the Peoples' Temple of Jim Jones, Sun Myang Moon, Bhagwan Shree Rajneesh – all are examples of the bizarre movements that attract, exploit, and destroy people in the name of God. And more will appear. The greater pity of it all is that such conduct in the name of religion repulses many honest souls who might otherwise learn the gospel and be saved (cf. 2 Pet. 2:2b).

Peter does not spare these subverters of the gospel. The Holy Spirit moved him to identify the true motives that underlie their deeds. They are morally perverse people, driven by covetousness. They are profiteering in the name of holiness, making merchandise of the trusting souls who follow them. And they are under sentence of destruction for their work's sake.

The Certain Fate of the Unrighteous

It seems to be the tendency of every wicked person to think that he is going to be an exception to the destruction which Peter has prophesied for all such folk. He sees others break the law and get caught but thinks that he is smart enough to get away with some crime; he knows that false teachers have been exposed and brought to nothing in the past but is confident that it will not happen to him. But notice how effectively this naive confidence is attacked by Peter. He argues that if God did not spare angels, cities, and even a whole race of men who deserved judgment for their sin, it is absurd to think that any one person is ever going to get away with an unrighteous subversion of the gospel of Christ.

> For if God did not spare angels when they sinned, but sent them to hell, putting them into gloomy dungeons to be held for judgment; if he did not spare the ancient world when he brought the flood on its ungodly people, but protected Noah, a preacher of righteousness, and seven others; if he condemned the cities of Sodom and Gomorrah by burning them to ashes, and made them an example of what is going to happen to the ungodly; and if he rescued Lot, a righteous man, who was distressed by the filthy lives of lawless men (for that righteous man, living among them day after day, was tormented in his righteous soul by the lawless deeds he saw and heard) – if this is so, then the Lord knows how to rescue godly men from trials and to hold the unrighteous for the day of judgment, while continuing their punishment (2 Pet. 2:4-9).

First, "God did not spare angels when they sinned, but sent them to hell." This is one of only two verses in the Bible which tell of the origin of Satan and his demonic host (cf. Jude 6). Satan was once an angel of heaven. But he instigated a rebellion against the authority of God and was cast out of that perfect place, along with the other angels who followed his lead.

Second, God "did not spare the ancient world when he brought the flood on its ungodly people." This is a reference to the judgment of the wicked generation of men who lived at the time of Noah. These ungodly people were given definite and clear warnings of coming destruction, but they scoffed at the notion of punishment and continued in their sinful ways –until the flood came.

Third, Peter recalls how God "condemned the cities of Sodom and Gomorrah by burning them to ashes" as another "example of what is going to happen to the ungodly." The Old Testament account of the destruction of these cities is found in Genesis 19:23-29. The scene described is one of absolute desolation. Fire and brimstone came from heaven to destroy all the impenitent people of those immoral cities and scorched the very earth itself until it was totally barren. The narrative ends by saying that "the smoke of the land went up as the smoke of a furnace."

Such examples could be multiplied. But these are sufficient to demonstrate man's basic responsibility of obedience to God. The godly person will be *delivered* from destruction; the unrighteous person will suffer *punishment* without mercy. No one is strong enough to fight God and win. False living produced by false teaching results in inevitable destruction.

A Description of the False Teachers

It is at this point that Peter goes into a detailed description of the nature of false teachers. Whether he has a specific group of false teachers of his own time in mind or is describing false teachers generally is difficult to say. Over a space of ten verses, he isolates six characteristics associated with the people he has in mind.

First, they are *sensual.* "This is especially true of those who follow the corrupt desire of the sinful nature and despise authority" (2 Pet. 2:10a). It is common for worldly people to yield to the lusts of their "sinful nature" (flesh, ASV) and to defile themselves with various impurities. It is the more reprehensible when such conduct is engaged in within the context of religion and with doctrines formulated to justify it.

In ancient Corinth, the goddess Aphrodite was worshiped by means of fornication in her temple. It was a doctrinal tenet of her cult that one could achieve spiritual union with the deity through physical union with one of her priestesses. In the late first century, there were already such teachers as Peter warned about here who were guilty of "turning the grace of our God into a license for immorality" (Jude 4) and teaching Christians that it was acceptable for them to be involved in "sexual immorality and the eating of food sacrificed to idols" (Rev. 2:20). Today we have the modern counterparts of these teachers in situation ethicists and the founders of religious communes where promiscuity is the norm.

Second, they are *arrogant* and unwilling to respect authority.

> Bold and arrogant, these men are not afraid to slander celestial beings; yet even angels, although they are stronger and more powerful, do not bring slanderous accusations against such beings in the presence of the Lord. But these men blaspheme in matters they do not understand. They are like brute beasts, creatures of instinct, born only to be caught and destroyed, and like beasts they too will perish.
>
> They will be paid back with harm for the harm they have done (2 Pet. 2:10b-13a).

Although the authority of Jesus Christ is perhaps the primary authority the apostle has in mind, it is surely the case that the people of whom he is speaking resist any form of authority that would restrain their sensual deeds. It is not insignificant that he likens such people to "brute beasts" and "creatures of instinct." The distinguishing mark of man in the animal world is his rationality. When this trait is sacrificed for the sake of unrestrained gratification of his instincts, the individual involved is living as a brute beast. He lives like an animal, and he gets caught in the snares which attract and destroy creatures who have no critical faculty of self-restraint.

Third, they are *self-indulgent* in their lifestyle. "Their idea of pleasure is to carouse in broad daylight. They are blots and blemishes, reveling in their pleasures while they feast with you" (2 Pet. 2:13b). With all concern for truth and righteousness gone, these false teachers become bolder in their sin. They behave shamefully, even when they are among the saints. Nothing inhibits them, for they have lost all semblance of self-respect.

106

Fourth, they are *lustful* and debased in heart. "With eyes full of adultery, they never stop sinning; they seduce the unstable" (2 Pet. 2:14a). The sensuous and self-indulgent lives these people lead are not enough to satisfy them. They are so addicted to carnal things that they "cannot cease from sin" (ASV). So every woman they see, even the virtuous woman who does nothing to encourage it, is an object of their lustful thoughts. She can be seen by these people only as a potential adulteress, and their fantasies engage her for such evil. And, of course, they are willing to seduce those whom they can in order to turn their evil dreams into reality.

Fifth, they are *covetous.*

> They are experts in greed – an accursed brood! They have left the straight way and wandered off to follow the way of Balaam son of Beor, who loved the wages of wickedness. But he was rebuked for his wrong-doing by a donkey – a beast without speech – who spoke with a man's voice and restrained the prophet's madness (2 Pet. 2:14b-16).

Peter has already called attention to this common trait of false teachers in verse three. They are experts in the deceitful practices of manipulating people for selfish advantage. Like Balaam (cf. Num. 22), they love the "wages of wickedness" and will do anything for money.

Sixth, they *prey on new converts and weak Christians.*

> These men are springs without water and mists driven by a storm. Blackest darkness is reserved for them. For they mouth empty, boastful words and, by appealing to the lustful desires of sinful human nature, they entice people who are just escaping from those who live in error. They promise them freedom, while they themselves are slaves of depravity – for a man is a slave to whatever has mastered him (2 Pet. 2:17-19).

Like clouds that seem to promise refreshing rain but give nothing, these false teachers make great boasts and are free with their promises. Especially do they promise "freedom" to their followers, i.e., an enlightened Christianity which does not worry itself with ethical boundaries and discipline. But how cruel is their sinful deception. They not only damn themselves but "people who are just escaping" from the old life of sin; they influence and lead astray those immature believers who have not yet fully developed to the point of being able to discern good and evil.

In connection with this section of text, you should read the book of Jude. There is a great deal of similarity (and possibly an element of dependence) between Jude and 2 Peter. Whether one writer was quoting the other or both men were reflecting a common oral or written source, they undoubtedly address themselves to the same issue of the danger to the church from false teachers.

Don't Turn Back!

For the sake of any among his readers who might have been attracted to such teachers already, Peter closes this section of his epistle with a warning against apostasy.

> If they have escaped the corruption of the world by knowing our Lord and Savior Jesus Christ and are again entangled in it and overcome, they are worse off at the end than they were at the beginning. It would have been better for them not to have known the way of righteousness, than to have known it and then to turn their backs on the sacred commandment that was passed on to them. Of them the proverbs are ture: "A dog returns to its vomit," and, "A sow that is washed goes back to her wallowing in the mud" (2 Pet. 2:20-22).

Yes, it is possible for a saved person (i.e., one who has "escaped the corruption of the world") to become "entangled" in sin again and "overcome." This frightening fact is supposed to be a warning against letting it happen. To make the warning even stronger, Peter says that people who fall away from Christ are worse off than those who never knew him. There are several New Testament passages which imply degrees of punishment (cf. Luke 12:47-48; Heb. 10:26). This passage lets us know that the most severe punishment of hell is reserved for the Christian who quits.

Conclusion

One writer has said that these words from Peter about false teachers constitute "the burning lava of the apostle's indignation." He is certainly correct in calling attention to their sin, their motives, and the consequences which will come both to them and their followers. He is merely building on the foundation already laid in other inspired writings.

While some think it is legalistic and unkind to insist on uniformity in the fundamental doctines of Christianity, such fears seem never to have deterred Peter and other early preachers. Their fear was not of exposing error but of failing to do so. They believed that God had spoken his will in the inscripturated Word and that his faithful Word was *something to hold on to.*

Chapter Thirteen

He Is Coming Again

2 Peter 3:1-18

If you were writing a letter to people who were suffering, what is the one thing above all others you would like to be able to say to them? It would likely be something like this: "What you are experiencing will not have been in vain. When this terrible ordeal is over, you will see that your suffering has made possible a joy and blessedness which otherwise could not have been known."

This reassuring message was given repeatedly to the earliest Christians. As they faced fierce trials of every sort, the message of God to them was to the effect that their faithfulness in these situations would be fully rewarded. Paul spoke of the fact that Christians "share in [Christ's] sufferings in order that we may also share in his glory." Then he added: "I consider that our present sufferings are not worth comparing with the glory that will be revealed in us" (Rom. 8:17-18). The same apostle told the saints at Corinth: "For our light and momentary troubles are achieving for us an eternal glory that far outweighs them all" (2 Cor. 4:17). And the apostle John recorded the resurrected Savior's words to the persecuted Christians at Smyrna:

Do not be afraid of what you are about to suffer. I tell you, the devil will put some of you in prison to test you, and you will suffer persecution for ten days. Be faithful, even to the point of death, and I will give you the crown of life (Rev. 2:10).

It should surprise no one to find Peter closing his second epistle to believers facing a time of struggle and persecution with a reminder that Jesus will one day come again.

He is coming to destroy the world, punish ungodly men, to usher faithful saints into heaven. There could be no more appropriate way to conclude his message. Be faithful! Hold on! The Lord is coming!

The Certainty of His Coming

The doctrine of the second coming of Christ has been an object of derision from the founding day of the church. Surely it is because the scoffers fear the Lord they have defied and do not want him to come back to judge their deeds. His return is an unpleasant thought to the man who has refused the truth, the unprepared man, the enemy of the cross. But it has never been the case that heaven needed the approval of men to carry out its sovereign purposes and promises.

In the Old Testament period the prophets spoke confidently of the *first* coming of Christ. As the years passed the hope of the people grew dim, and they began to doubt the promise of God. Then, when the Son of God came in the "fulness of time," they did not receive him. In a similar way, the New Testament prophets have spoken confidently of the *second* coming of Christ. But because he did not return in a matter of a few months or years from the time the promise was made, men began to doubt it. History is repeating itself. Thus Peter wrote:

Dear friends, this is now my second letter to you. I have written both of them as reminders to stimulate you to wholesome thinking. I want you to recall the words spoken in the past by the holy prophets and the command given by our Lord and Savior through your apostles.

First of all, you must understand that in the last days scoffers will come, scoffing and following their own evil desires. They will say, "Where is this 'coming' he promised? Ever since our fathers died, everything goes on as it has since the beginning of creation." But they deliberately forget that long ago by God's word the heavens existed and the earth was formed out of water and with water. By water also the world of that time was deluged and destroyed. By the same word the present heavens and earth are reserved for fire, being kept for the day of judgment and destruction of ungodly men (2 Pet. 3:1-7).

If this reaffirmation of the certainty of the return of Jesus was needed even in the first Christian century, how much more is it needed now. Several years ago two sociologists from the University of California at Berkeley did a sampling of religious beliefs among "church-going Americans." One of the questions asked was "Do you believe Jesus will actually return to the earth some day?" Only 44 percent of the Protestants answered with a definite affirmative; 47 percent of the Catholics surveyed gave a "definitely" response. Given the facts that this survey did not include anyone but "church-going Americans" (and therefore was a narrowed sampling of our total population) and was taken almost two decades ago, it is apparent that our generation mocks the idea that Jesus is coming again.

In the first century, men were poking fun at the second coming on the basis of a philosophical presupposition called *uniformitarianism*. They said, "Where is this 'coming' he promised? Ever since our fathers died, everything goes on as it has since the beginning of creation" (2 Pet. 3:4). It is the same philosophical position which is at the root of unbelief today. Supernaturalism is ruled out by such a world view. The universe is held to be a closed system, and all things within it must be explained by purely natural phenomena. This is why Jesus could not have been born of a virgin. This is why he could not have been raised bodily from the dead. This is why he could not come again and raise the dead. Everything from comparative religions to the theory of evolution rests on this philosophic premise.

Uniformitarianism is a woefully inadequate thesis. It deliberately refuses to face a world of hard facts and impossible (given its position) problems. For example, suppose we assume for the sake of argument that natural law, as we observe it functioning in the universe, is all there is to reality. Where did the substance of the universe come from originally? Natural law is adequate to tell us how certain elements combine and function under certain conditions, but it cannot tell us how those elements got here in the first place.

Peter referred to another fact which the uniformitarians deliberately ignore. What about the great flood – which is attested not only in Scripture but in non-biblical sources as well? That event demonstrates that things do not always proceed without interruption in this world.

Yes, Jesus is coming again. We have his own word in the matter. He told the apostles, "And if I go and prepare a place for you, I will come back and take you to be with me that you also may be where I am" (John 14:3). There was no doubt or hesitation. He promised confidently, "I will come back."

Then there is the word of angels to the effect that Jesus will come again. When the Lord was taken up to heaven from the Mount of Olives near Jerusalem, two angels appeared and spoke to the apostles who had witnessed the ascension. As they were looking into the heavens, two men appeared and spoke to them. They promised: "This same Jesus, who has been taken from you into heaven, will come back in the same way you have seen him go into heaven" (Acts 1:10-11).

There are numerous statements made by the Holy Spirit through the prophets and evangelists of the church.

For the Lord himself will come down from heaven, with a loud command, with the voice of the archangel and with the trumpet call of God, and the dead in Christ will rise first. After that, we who are still alive and are left will be caught up together with them in the clouds to meet the Lord in the air. And so we will be with the Lord forever. Therefore encourage one another with these words (1 Thess. 4:16-18).

Just as man is destined to die once, and after that to face judgment, so Christ was sacrificed once to take away the sins of many people; and he will appear a second time, not to bear sin, but to bring salvation to those who are waiting for him (Heb. 9:27-28).

The promise of the Word of God is clear. Either Christ is coming again, or there is no reason to believe anything written in the New Testament. And if one accepts any part of that book, by what right and on what reasonable basis does he reject those statements about the second coming? *Jesus is coming again!*

The Circumstances of His Return

Men may not keep their promises, but God does. Jesus is coming again, and the passing of time does not dim the divine memory or resolve.

But do not forget this one thing, dear friends: With the Lord a day is like a thousand years, and a thousand years are like a day. The Lord is not slow in keeping his promise, as some understand slowness. He is patient with you, not wanting anyone to perish, but everyone to come to repentance (2 Pet. 3:8-9).

How ironic! The delay of Jesus about his coming is designed to demonstrate divine patience and compassion. It is calculated to give men time to repent and prepare for his arrival. But many misunderstand his patience and use the passing time to their own evil ends rather than in righteousness and anticipation. It must have been the same in Noah's day. As he built the ark and preached repentance, men surely grew bolder in their mockery of the God-fearing preacher. We must preach about the return of Christ to our sinful generation and plead for repentance. If we must be ridiculed for doing so, so be it.

> But the day of the Lord will come like a thief. The heavens will disappear with a roar; the elements will be destroyed by fire, and the earth and everything in it will be laid bare (2 Pet. 3:10).

Most will be caught off guard when the Lord returns. Everything will be "business as usual" on that day. The warnings and appeals of Scripture are the only announcements of the second coming to be given. There will be no special eye-opening event in advance of his return which will convince the scoffers and let all men know the time of his arrival. Contrary to the teachings of many, that day will not have been predicted by modern "prophets" who will have called the world to a state of righteous anticipation. "For in the days before the flood, people were eating and drinking, marrying and giving in marriage, up to the day Noah entered the ark; and they knew nothing about what would happen until the flood came and took them all away. That is how it will be at the coming of the Son of Man" (Matt. 24:38-39).

Believers live with the knowledge of Jesus' second coming in their hearts constantly. "No one knows about that day or hour, not even the angels in heaven, nor the Son, but only the Father. Be on guard! Be alert! You do not know when that time will come" (Mark 13:32-33). So we live soberly and righteously. We watch and pray. We stay busy doing the will of God. Whenever the Lord appears to our view, we shall rejoice at this presence and stand before him in confidence.

From passages other than our text, we can know that the following things will occur when he returns.

First, a great noise will mark his arrival and the end of time. "For the Lord himself shall descend from heaven, with a shout, with the voice of the archangel, and with the trump of God" (1 Thess. 4:16a ASV).

Second, the dead will all be raised. "Do not be amazed at this, for a time is coming when all who are in their

116

graves will hear his voice and come out – those who have done good will rise to live, and those who have done evil will rise to be condemned" (John 5:28-29).

Third, those still alive on earth at his coming will be changed. "Listen, I tell you a mystery: We will not all sleep, but we will all be changed – in a flash, in the twinkling of an eye, at the last trumpet. For the trumpet will sound, the dead will be raised imperishable, and we will all be changed" (1 Cor. 15:51-52).

Fourth, the final Judgment will occur.

> Then I saw a great white throne and him who was seated on it. Earth and sky fled from his presence, and there was no place for them. I saw the dead, great and small, standing before the throne, and books were opened. Another book was opened, which is the book of life. The dead were judged according to what they had done as recorded in the books (Rev. 20:11-12).

Fifth, the righteous and the wicked will be separated and given their places of eternal abode.

> And he shall set the sheep on his right hand, but the goats on the left. Then shall the King say unto them on his right hand, Come ye blessed of my Father, inherit the kingdom prepared for you from the foundation of the world ... Then shall he say also unto them on the left hand, depart from me, ye cursed, into the eternal fire which is prepared for the devil and his angels (Matt. 25:33-34, 41 ASV).

Returning now to our text, we also know that the earth will "be destroyed (dissolved, ASV) by fire" and "be laid bare." This is not a fire of renovation and purging but a fire of destruction. There will be no human life on earth following the return of Christ – not for a thousand years or even a single day – for planet earth will pass from existence. The future life of the saints will be in a totally new world from this one.

Since everything will be destroyed in this way, what kind of people ought you to be? You ought to live holy and godly lives as you look forward to the day of God and speed its coming. That day will bring about the destruction of the heavens by fire, and the elements will melt in the heat. But in keeping with his promise we are looking forward to a new heaven and a new earth, the home of righteousness (2 Pet. 3:11-13).

Appeals Based on the Second Coming

What thought should come to mind as one thinks about the return of the Lord? "So then, dear friends, since you are looking forward to this, make every effort to be found spotless, blameless and at peace with him" (2 Pet. 3:14).

Specifically, Peter urged his Christian readers to view the longsuffering of God in the proper light. In verse nine he referred to the fact that unbelievers misinterpret the passing of time between the promise of the second coming and its fulfillment. But Christians are to see this time in proper perspective.

Bear in mind that our Lord's patience means salvation, just as our dear brother Paul also wrote you with the wisdom that God gave him. He writes the same way in all his letters, speaking in them of these matters. His letters contain some things that are hard to understand, which ignorant and unstable people distort, as they do the other Scriptures, to their own destruction (2 Pet. 3:15-16).

The reference here to the writings of Paul is interesting. Paul wrote frequently about the second coming, and the apostle to the Jews appealed to his colleague's writings for confirmation of what he had been saying. This shows, among other things, that the writings of Paul were already being circulated widely and were regarded as "Scripture" (i.e., God-breathed writings, cf. 2 Tim. 3:16-17).

The tendency of men to pervert the statements of the

Bible relevent to the second coming (and other themes) is still evident today. What Peter said was being done with the writings of Paul in his own time is still being done in our time. It is not enough to have an inspired document in one's possession; that document must be respected as authoritative and studied by the canons of reason. It is an awesome responsibility to have the Word of God in one's possession. It must be interpreted carefully and lived courageously.

> Therefore, dear friends, since you already know this, be on your guard so that you may not be carried away by the error of lawless men and fall from your secure position" (2 Pet. 3:17).

We know of the approaching end of time and appearance of Jesus. We have not been left in darkness on this topic so that it could overtake us to our detriment (cf. 1 Thess. 5:4-5a). Indeed, let us use the time wisely until he does appear.

> But grow in the grace and knowledge of our Lord and Savior Jesus Christ. To him be glory both now and forever! Amen (2 Pet. 3:18).

Paul said, "But since we belong to the day, let us be self-controlled, putting on faith and love as a breastplate, and the hope of salvation as a helmet" (1 Thess. 5:8).

Conclusion

The first Christians did not fear the return of Christ; they looked forward to it and prayed for its arrival. They even used a short prayer for its occurrence in their common greetings. They met and parted with the Aramaic *Marana tha* (cf. 1 Cor. 16:22). It means: "Come, O Lord!"

May we, too, come to have such a positive attitude toward that day. May we long for it and see it as a day to be desired. May our confidence in Christ be so firm that we shall see Jesus' promise to come again as *something to hold on to*.